Fun Schway,
the North American way

Fun Schway,
the North American way

The Mystical Movement of Energy
Feng Shui

Mallory Neeve Wilkins

IIDA, ASID, IDC, ARIDO

To a balanced life & healthy home — all the best!! Mallory

iUniverse, Inc.

New York Bloomington Shanghai

Fun Schway, the North American way
The Mystical Movement of Energy Feng Shui

Copyright © 2008 by Mallory Neeve Wilkins

iUniverse books may be ordered through booksellers or by contacting:

iUniverse
1663 Liberty Drive
Bloomington, IN 47403
www.iuniverse.com
1-800-Authors (1-800-288-4677)

Because of the dynamic nature of the Internet, any Web addresses or links contained in this book may have changed since publication and may no longer be valid.

The views expressed in this work are solely those of the author and do not necessarily reflect the views of the publisher, and the publisher hereby disclaims any responsibility for them.

ISBN: 978-0-595-48273-3 (pbk)
ISBN: 978-0-595-60359-6 (ebk)

Printed in the United States of America

Dedicated

To

Mabelle

Joey

Muff

Contents

Introduction xi

Inspiration 1

Surroundings 23

Elements 39

Awareness 63

Relationships 81

Knowledge 107

Attraction 119

Cleansing 135

Wisdom 145

Questions and Answers 149

The Mystical Movement of Energy

The ancient art of living in harmony with your environment.

The Triangle Evolves

The GREAT ABSOLUTE = *Formless Substance*

is an essence which is undivided.

This *Silence* (static) produced *Formless Intelligence,*

the Creator, which is your inner *Intuition.*

Your thoughts create

and your ideas become *Form.*

Another sees your *Form* (ideas)

From their *Formless Substance* (silence)

comes *Formless Intelligence* (creation-intuition)

and their thoughts and ideas become *Form*

Another sees their *Form*

—and—

The Triangle Evolves.

FENG SHUI

the mystical movement of unseen energy

Creation never ending.

Introduction

Ancient history, alchemy, science, philosophy, and the mystical movement of energy are all part of an ongoing quest for a deeper understanding of life.

What happens when things go wrong, bad luck and mishaps keep coming your way? This means there is a lack of balance from deep within the ancient mystical flow of positive and negative energy within your environment. Loss and change will improve with corrections, in your health, relationships, career, creativity and finances.

Today, many popular television programs, books, CDs, and other sources offer inspiration, self-help, health, and creative solutions for an overall sense of well-being. My purpose in this book is to help you understand and locate *your* positive energy by unfolding the secrets of the mystical movement of energy within and around you.

By taking a closer look at your home and environment, you will see that the way you treat your place is a direct reflection of how others treat you. You need to understand how to change negative to positive energy within yourself, as well as in your environment.

Popular home improvement programs offer ways to enhance your lifestyle, home, and surroundings with creative designs and healthier ways to live. We add this, take away that, and suddenly feel better ... Feng Shui energy.

From many years of designing, planning, teaching, and working with energy, knowledgeable solutions are recommended for a healthier environment filled with prosperity and positive energy. It is not a science, philosophy, or religion. It is a fact of life! The following theories and short stories offer numerous secret enhancements of the elements for everyday practice. You can read over three hundred guidelines and questions and answers to improve your lifestyle the North American way, through the ancient art of living in harmony with the environment. Fun Schway!

But Grannie ...

Why are you cleaning and painting Daddy's garage?

Because Daddy's finances are not very good and his garage is very messy. If we clean up the garage and wash the car, we will watch and see things get better for him. The garage is in the Wealth area of this home. All his tools and garden things have to be put in order so it looks cared for. We will change the negative energy to positive energy.

Why did you move Baby Lindsay's crib?

The baby is twisting, turning, and crying too much. She is almost completely turned around in her crib. Her little body is automatically trying to move into its best energy field. She should have her head facing north and we will see her settle down as this is her best direction for health.

Why are we taking our shoes off to walk in the grass?

We all need to be in contact with nature, feel the sun on our heads, feel the ground beneath our feet, and feel the breath of the planet brush against our cheeks. We need to eat our fruits and vegetables. I like to drink water that has sat in the sun for three hours because it has been enhanced with light. By doing this we are nurturing our bodies.

Where did you get all those old books, Grannie?

Not so long ago in the 1970s, in a country called China, there was a rebellion against their ancient heritage traditions and a book called the *I Ching*. The people thought that if they got rid of such beliefs they would be more accepted by modern-day cultures, so they destroyed most of their ancient treasures and writings. Some that remained were taken to England, Japan, and San Francisco. These are my collections of the ancient Feng Shui teachings.

INSPIRATION

Change comes to those who become detached.

Be silent. Still the mind.

Be a choiceless watcher of your environment—

One who only hears and sees.

A new vibrant energy rises to the surface.

A new awareness.

Everything is alive, connected, and changing
and your feelings toward different colors, shapes, and elements will alter
from year to year because of the Earth's electromagnetic field. Take
note!

Feng Shui (the energy movement of wind and water)
was once called *Kan Yu,* meaning cover and support, reflecting above
and below or heaven and earth concepts. These are from the *I Ching,* or
"Book of Changes," first collected nearly five thousand years ago.

Feng Shui knowledge is from the ancient compass school study
or classic teaching, with a five-thousand-year-old history. New studies,
like Black Hat Sect (Tibetan/Buddhist), were created for the United
States in 1984, and do not conform with the full concepts of the ancient
traditional teachings.

The way you treat your home is a direct reflection of the way you are
treated by others.

Free-flowing energy is a river stocked with gifts.
Learn to see and have an eye for details. Remove blockages.

Energy is the breath of the planet.
It is the momentum of life which circulates through everything.
Cleanse your environment by removing all damaged, cracked, or broken
things.

Universal Law is said to be an interwoven life energy
made up of both good-luck Yang and bad-luck Yin, ever creating the
ups and downs. Write a list of your life's path of ups and downs.

Yin and Yang is the theory of opposites.
The Yin side of the building would not be as bright as the Yang side.
Where are you most comfortable?

Yin and Yang colors
Yin is the dark side. On a scale of one to ten, with ten being black, Yin equals levels six to ten. The Yang color spectrum is from one to five.

Personalized energy
You carry the energy of your birth year throughout your life. The energy of your birth year affects your moods, likes and dislikes, friendships, creativity, and health. Take 1980 for example. This year carries the energy of a Yang Metal year. Other specifications calculated on the Energy charts for a female born in this year are: her Pa Kua is #4; she would carry energy of an East person with positive energy locations of north, east, south, and southeast; and, the zodiac animal would be Monkey with positive energy numbers of 9, 4, 3, and 1. (This is unless she was born early in the year before the Chinese year changed. The readings are different for a male born in the same year.) The section on Elements will explain this further.

Enhance your aura (the energy shimmer that surrounds your body) and positive energy with a smile, whenever. Luck and good fortune are founded on politeness, charity, and giving kindness whenever possible.

Feng Shui is the use of natural products.

Energy flow and its movement
is affected by weather, temperature, wind, storms, rain, and snow, and is transmitted through media sounds, light, and heat. Take note of your environment and its changes.

Thank Your Lucky Stars!

Good luck and good fortune are cosmic stardusts that dance around the environment in an invisible state. That is what I was told many years ago. Here is a list of a few considerations to ponder.

A dog hears things that we don't hear. Many animals see things we don't see. In another dimension, there is a deeper awareness. Music can reach a pitch that is not heard by humans, yet many creatures can hear it.

Daydreaming can pass time, as we drive from one place to another without any recollection of the actual drive. There are many mysteries.

How a tree of over one hundred feet in height developed from a minute seed is overwhelming to think about. Where did that power come from for its growth and strength, and why does it not just fall over in hurricanes, blizzards and great winds?

The energy within us all is the same energy that boosts and opens those tiny seeds into mighty forests. How? Nature provides it from within the earth (yin energy). At a particular temperature (fire energy), with just the right moisture (water energy), a current develops, and bingo! The breath, the wind, the power develop, and from a dead-looking tree of winter blossom millions of buds into leaves: alchemy.

Human beings are Yang while the planet Earth is Yin, and if humans can incorporate this Yin energy, possibilities are endless.

This inner earth energy is what makes us grow, developing wisdom. Within our quiet times in a nature setting, we can feel or hear it. Our intuition from the Great Absolute comes forth, nurturing our growth with truth. It can be difficult to do, but relax, walk in the country. Be in the quiet and listen. Stare deeply at nature, focus on something that appeals to your senses, and a new light within comes to you.

Good fun schway … says Grannie!

Youthful Thinking

I enjoy teaching. One afternoon class for a group of parents was marked on my studio calendar for a Monday in May. I arrived at the school to be greeted by several grade-two students. They informed me that I would be talking to their moms and dads in their classroom. A couple of them wanted to know if it would be okay if they could help me. They led the way as I followed them through the halls to the second floor of the renovated 1948 brick building.

We entered their classroom, already set up awaiting my arrival. Josh introduced himself and his friend Aaron. I opened my portfolio and withdrew my magic markers in many colors. They liked that. A large flow chart was located at the front of the classroom.

"What are you going to do first?" Josh asked as I began to draw a large circle.

Another student in a white eyelet cotton dress approached with curious eyes. She announced she was called Betty, but her real name was Elizabeth. Her silky skin was a soft, milk chocolate color and she had incredible, large hazel eyes that sparkled with enthusiasm.

"What's that you are drawing?" Betty asked.

"Hmmm, what does it look like to you?" I replied with a smile.

"The moon," she responded. I continued with the Yin-Yang symbol, separating the circle into two sections.

"No!" burst out Josh. "It's the earth, right?"

"What's that *S* letter for in the middle of your circle?" asked Aaron impatiently. I continued by producing the Yin and Yang symbol, coloring the left side dark, leaving a small open white circle in the middle, then placing the same small circle on the right white side and coloring it black.

"Oh … it's the earth full of black and white people, right?" announced Josh. "It looks like a little bit of each mixed together, right?"

"Well, kids, it is actually a drawing indicating the balance of dark and light. You know about opposites? There is good and bad, or perhaps hot and cold, up and down, night and day … so this indicates that the earth is in harmony. You can see that there is a little dark in the light section and a little white circle on the dark side." I paused.

"You mean there is a little good in the bad, and a little bad in the good," Josh pointed out excitedly.

"What do you think, Betty?" I asked, smiling.

"I see more dark than light. Maybe there is more bad than good. Maybe the S shape that separates them is for Satan?"

You just never know what-the-devil comes out of the mouths of kids!

I pulled out some black sheets of paper and asked them to place one on each desk. With a little pushing, they accomplished the task.

"What's this for?" asked Aaron.

"I am going to show your parents how to see their aura."

None of the children spoke, but each had an inquisitive eye, waiting for me to say something. Several minutes passed before Josh asked for the "o-raw" to be explained.

"You and me, and everybody else, are full of energy," I said looking and pointing at each one individually.

"I know," Aaron jumped in. "My grandpa tells me that all the time. He tells me I have too much energy." I couldn't help but laugh.

"Well, your energy can be seen all around you … like a soft shimmer or glow." Their eyes widened, like I was going to produce magic for them. "Here, take a black piece of paper and put it on the desk." The three children quickly scrambled to find a place to sit near me, and got themselves ready for the next step.

I held my hands up shaking my fingers loosely. They instinctively copied my gestures before I showed or asked them to do the same.

"This will activate your energy. Now, show me your two pointing fingers, next to your thumb. That's good." I showed them how to point the fingers together, fingernail to fingernail inches above the piece of black paper, so that they would look at the inside of their hand with the index fingers pointing, and the other fingers curled in towards their palm, with their thumbs pointing upwards.

"Now don't let the two fingers touch. There must be a small space between them." The children had it down pat. I helped them align their hands just so.

I told them to stare down between the two pointing fingers onto the black paper for a moment without blinking their eyes. Then they would slowly pull the fingers apart, and they would notice a shadow left from where their fingers had been, lingering over the black paper.

"Did you see that stream of mist?" The children all nodded, and started chatting amongst themselves about this trick. "Well, that mist is your personal aura. Sometimes it may be a colored mist. And sometimes, when you are very relaxed and calm, staring at a person, you may see this shimmer of light all around their head or body. What you are actually seeing … is the energy of that person."

"Can I see my own body energy?" asked seven-year-old Josh.

"Sure," I responded, "but you will have to stare hard at yourself in the mirror." The children played with this idea for several minutes and pretended to see each other's energy.

"This is so much fun!" exclaimed Betty after a few successes.

"Do you know some more stuff?" Josh inquired jumping to his feet.

I finished drawing an outline of an eight-sided compass on the flip chart, setting my marker on the ledge nearby.

"Would you like to *feel* your energy?" And they rambunctiously scattered around. I couldn't help but laugh at their enthusiasm. "Okay, settle down. It won't work if you get all excited." They stood remarkably still.

I began rubbing my hands together, and before I could explain anything they began mimicking my actions. After fifteen seconds or so, I loosely separated my hands about four to six inches apart, letting the fingers relax, as if holding a ball and moving the hands back and forth ever so slightly without touching.

"You will feel an invisible cushion, like a cotton ball. This soft pressure you feel is your energy that you have activated. You are now feeling what you saw on the black piece of paper, that stream of mist."

"Cool!" exclaimed Aaron.

"Remember, kids. When you are happy, full of joy and love, you have a big, bright energy field. When you are sad, hurt, or hateful, you have small, dark energy. So be full of fun and laughter, and you will attract good fortune."

It wasn't long before the parents came into the classroom to hear me speak about the "mystical movement of energy." I allowed the young students to begin the program with their demonstrations and drawing of the Yin and Yang symbol. The children were amazing and so excited. When it came time to sit, all three tiptoed to the back of the room and waited patiently during my hour-long talk, never making a sound, eager to learn another fact of life.

Good fun schway … says Grannie!

Feng Shui is an awareness of things, places, and people that offend or are a bother. Identify your awareness of all unpleasant things and situations by keeping a record of this information.

Poison arrows
are referred to as sharp, pointed edges, pointing in our direction, such as the corner edge of a wall, a filing cabinet corner, furniture edges, overhead beams, satellite dishes, etc.

Feng Shui energy travels in a curve.
It is meandering. Identify straight-line paths in your environment, as this is identified as a poison arrow, referring to a direct attack which threatens to wound.

Feng Shui is an awareness art.
When making any corrections to your environment, it should always be recorded in a journal and written with your intent for improvement. It can take three weeks to three months, and other times three days.

Feng Shui advises
that too large or too many windows allow for vulnerability of the occupants.

Feng Shui cautions
that no one should sit with their back to the entry door of a room, especially when sitting at a desk or eating. If there is no alternative, place a mirror nearby so you always are in control of who or what is behind you.

Missing areas
When something is missing from your life, look closely at the shape and floor plan (design) of your building and see where there is lack, or missing areas which need restoring, fixing, or cleansing.

Placement for energy movement
is created by setting up rooms so that no chair or sofa has its back to any
doorway, blocking the incoming calming flow of energy.

Placement needs complete organization,
as open shelves are negative because of their cutting-edge shelves. Display items (mixed) into groupings so energy can move throughout the
space; never overcrowd shelves. Any sharp edges are pointed corners
representing weapons. Doors on shelves are more protective.

Placement
Sofas should not be stacked with pillows, closing all opportunities for
the new to enter. By keeping one side open, you're not blocking new
opportunities.

Placement for art
is recommended two to three inches apart when combining items on a
wall.

Placement of ceiling fixtures
like chandeliers, require a thirty-inch space above an eating table in a
room with eight-foot ceilings; and, thirty-six inches above the table in a
room with nine-foot ceiling height.

Interior flow is best with round edges,
which are more conducive to smooth-flowing energy, when selecting
furniture.

Feng Shui dictates balance
and an adequate distance between conversational seating, which is eight
feet (knee to knee) for easy energy movement.

Negative energy cleanse
is needed for protection from waste products, dirty clothes, etc. These kinds of things should always be covered, or located under tables or behind a closet door, to help control the damaging flow within a sleep or work space.

Stagnant energy
can be found when an item that is not touched, used, or loved turns negative and spreads its energy throughout the space. Take a walk through each room, having an eye for detail, once a month and remove such unused items.

Sports Trauma

Springtime is when we are supposed to throw open the windows, move the furniture, scrub down, toss out, and get rid of old baggage. It wasn't until June that I finally got my act together to undertake this yearly task.

There was freshness in the morning breeze. I was ready to begin with the second floor closets. I had three large garbage bags set to one side. One was marked "throw aways," another marked "keep items," and a third marked "not sure." The third bag was for items that were "maybes" but couldn't get back into the closet if they were not loved, needed or used regularly. The idea was that if they were not used within the past five months, they were not needed, and if they were loved, they would have been used, so to speak.

Whenever one does a space cleansing using Feng Shui techniques, one should combine the five natural elements together and play your favorite music while working. I have an old silver tray (metal) where I place a wooden candle holder (wood), with a red candle (fire) and small amount of ocean water in a clear glass container (water), next to a quartz crystal (earth). You can purchase these types of kits already put together, but I find it is more enhancing if you consider the five elements and make up your own personal one to use whenever clearing out old energies, like after a nasty quarrel or burnt dinner. The idea of the energy clearing kit is so you activate the five elements as you clean out the negative energy. Light the candle and pour out some water, etc.

During this particular exercise, I passed by my son's room while fetching the vacuum, and casually looked in, noticing the long empty wall across from the entry door. I commented to him that something should be hung on it, as there wasn't even a window and it just appeared to be lacking something. He must use his own energy to do any clean-up or changes. I continued with what I was doing.

Within a few hours, my closet was emptied. It was washed down, vacuumed, and any disrepair was fixed. My choice of Cat Stevens music might not have appealed to my teenagers, but it did the trick for me. I hung up red coat hangers, because my birth year energy is Yin Fire, all matching, while any others were discarded. (It is suggested to leave 10 percent of the hangers empty, so that you are always ready for new to come into your life.) I figured I could use some prosperity and good luck, so I left 15 percent empty.

The closet is usually the first and last space we are in before bed and first thing in the morning, so we want to make sure we pick up positive energy to begin or end our day. It is refreshing to sense the calmness of an organized space. All clothes should be organized in color groups.

I placed everything white and with beige tones together; another section had dark tones of black, browns, etc. The colors were kept together in color groups so not to be mixed. It all appeared very orderly.

Nothing should be on the floor unless contained in a box, basket, or mat. If an article hasn't been used within the last five months, remove it or get rid of it. It should not be there becoming stagnant when not being used, or touched. *Stagnant* is a strong negative. Another important note is that no space should ever be jammed or crowded.

Within a few days, I had completed all the upper-level closets. I was gathering my seven bags (amazing how things accumulate) of stuff to get rid of, when I once again passed by the bedroom of my son, the cyclist-surfer athlete, noticing that he had placed a couple of his cycling shirts on the wall behind the head of his bed. This was not a good idea. I intended to mention this to him.

The head of the bed must be kept clear so all positive energy reaches you during sleep. You do not want anything negative nearby, especially over your head.

It was a busy time of year for both surfing and biking, as competitions had begun. He was in Whistler for a Trials event. (This extreme cycling sport was very popular on the west coast at that time.)

The following week, all my bags of worldly collections had been distributed to either Big Brother or Women in Need organizations. It is always best to give anything you can away. If you can sell it on eBay or Craigslist, all the better for your pocketbook.

Another day passed and my daughter brought up the fact that her brother had something over the head of his bed. "Did you not know that he had done this?" she inquired. The opportunity had not arisen for me to mention it to him. Later that very evening we got a phone call from the hospital. He was in the emergency room getting stitches from an event mishap.

Trials is definitely an extreme sport of bike riding with obstacle climbing, jumping, and trick performing that can often cause accidents if the rider is not totally focused. This time, his scraped arms, bloody nose, and scarred legs were topped off with stitches to the chin. Of course, it is never bad enough to rethink the sport. It just adds to the challenge, so I am told.

We joked, that he should have known better than to attract negative energy to his sport and to himself by doing such a thing. When corrections are to be made, they should be made by the person himself, not someone else, for maximum benefit; and in this case, they certainly needed to be made.

After a few days of rest and a lecture from his sister, he removed the shirts from above his bed. It's not that it didn't look pretty cool, but with all the Feng Shui techniques around our home, he should have known better. She had taken one look at his wall, pointed the finger at the shirts, and shook her head. He got the hint.

We are always warned to remove anything from over the bed, and keep the energy calm and clear around the head when sleeping. It's a health issue. A strong headboard is recommended for the bed for support. We must make sure that the incoming positive energy is not distracted, so that our sleep is peaceful. This clarity can help keep our memory sharp. Reflective surfaces are the worst. No mirrors are allowed. When the energy hits the item, it can turn negative before it reaches the one asleep; therefore, the negative energy could have easily influenced the cycling accident.

The bedroom is very important to keep free from clutter for good health and prosperity. Nothing on the floor or under the bed is another caution for better health. We spend more hours in this room than any other.

Another day, another look into the athlete's bedroom; a handsome Trials poster was situated over his desk, several feet from his bed. The new location was much better. It filled some of the long empty wall that had bothered me in the first place, and now gave him an identity in his favorite sport. Or was it surfing? Just remember to keep your head free from obstructions overhead.

Good fun schway … says Grannie!

Feng Shui is a balance of Yin and Yang,
so that every space should represent calm with no clutter, and all things
contained (in pots, baskets, trays, etc.) for maximum abundance and a
sense of well-being.

Body balance energy is an organic system.
The *I Ching* ("Book of Changes") began explaining five thousand years
ago that there are as many internal changes as there are environmental
changes.

Feng Shui warns against using octagon shapes
in the interior of buildings. Beware.

Electronics are metal elements
and operate best in the west area of a room, especially when placed next
to something round.

Feng Shui warns
of straight lines causing negative energy flow because they flow too
quickly (corridors, hallways, etc.). Energy paths should meander gently.
The art of placement is important.

Just as life itself evolves,
changes in your residence, favorite colors, apparel, etc., are necessary
because routine causes stagnant energy. (Not any different than changing fashion trends, nor nature with its seasonal changes: nor history,
with the constant relocation of ancient tribes from place to place.)

Every space carries different energy.
A boardroom differs from a spa, a kitchen differs from a bedroom. Be
conscious of these differences and of how you feel in each space you
enter. Some rooms you are attracted to, while others you don't go into
very much.

Feng Shui energy change is accomplished
through color, shapes, or an element item (e.g., fire equals lamp) which
can actually introduce significant changes; changing a table from square
to round, or a wall from beige to green.

Longevity in ancient days
was enhanced by peaches in still-life and deer in artwork, or by pine and
bamboo in landscapes, or by chrysanthemums.

Natural items
such as light, sound, and music can enhance and encourage positive
energy to any Aspiration sector of a room when just the right level is
found.

Remedies
Natural elements are preferred in healthy environments; replace all
dried (past six months) and plastic flowers with silk or growing plants.

Everything is made up of energy.
Wash your car regularly and notice how it always runs and looks better.

Things that stimulate energy
are: a) objects with shiny surfaces, b) flags, and c) color.

Art
Family photos belong in the Southwest sector of a room (the Aspiration
Relationship section) for enhancement and improvement.

Relationships
Truthful communication is the way to improve relationships and should
be done only when you are facing your best direction (from your personal Pa Kua chart) for positive results.

Energy flow into a room from the entry door
flows straight ahead, deflecting off the wall across the room. It is never
wise to sit directly in the path of incoming energy. Let it slow down
first or you can become anxious.

Zen rooms are calm spaces without electronics and high energy colors,
but they should contain all the five natural elements for harmony and
balance.

Mirrors
are never recommended in places of business, except for retail establish-
ments. It is an item that has to be considered carefully.

Electronic clutter
is a combination of excessive wires, cords, and plugs. It must be contained and hidden from incoming energy flow so as not to weaken it.

Change is good.
Activate energy by moving accessories regularly (changing art, pillows,
table-top decor, mantle displays, wall groupings, etc.). Keep things
fresh.

Less is best
If you don't love it or use it, get rid of it; the incoming energy will only
enhance something you don't want. It will only aggravate you, like
hanging onto old baggage that just will not go away.

Smooth going
Things in your life flow smoothly when you are situated in your personal best space. Know and remember your personal four best locations
for positive energy.

Your home is a reflection
of who you are and your inner personality. Look around. Remove all
energy blocks.

Personal items
such as your favorite books can be visible when placed decoratively on
shelves, in baskets, or stacked to raise a low lamp for better reading.

Be mindful
of your personal space and aware of its energy. Make just one alteration
to your space and watch for feedback into your life (journal it) before
you introduce another correction.

Beware of dark buildings.
Different environments suit different types of people. Realtors know
this better than most; closed houses are Yin energy (dark) and everyone
that enters brings in Yang (from the outside) energy along with their
own energy pattern, either positive or negative. Cleanse with candles if
you have a bad reaction after visitors have departed.

Continuity brings harmony.
Balance a room's color, furniture placement, and five elements with
upper and lower items, such as crown moldings (high) and carpets
(low).

Reflective surfaces magnify the energy flow.
They (glass, mirrors) are well placed when located in a dining room, as
it magnifies nurturing foods. Reflective surfaces in a bedroom activate
the energy when a calmness is required. Each room provides a different
effect on the occupant's needs and health.

Beauty
A single item of beauty can attract more abundance and correction into
your life than having many items. Less is best.

Connection to past
Always remove items that hold connection to past difficulties. Light
candles while making new adjustments. No past baggage is allowed
while you focus on new and prosperous ventures, relationships, or
creativities.

Keep yourself positive
by preparing your clothes the night before. This starts the energy flow
and control as a decision has already been made before rising.

Dark Yin days are brightened
by wearing the color yellow somewhere; adding yellow flowers to a
room; or listening to or watching comedies, which are good remedies
for the blues.

Keep yourself positive
by identifying deep rooted problems by writing to yourself or to another
person. The problems must be released from within to cleanse the clutter from the body. Cleansing the outer environment is just half of the
problem correction. Cleanse your inner self (this harmonizes Yin and
Yang energies) after you have done your environment because the outside energy effects your inner energy.

Not coping well with life's changes
can come from having too much black (water element) as one seeks the
dark—winter. Add touches of red (fire color) or white (metal color) to
your space or to your wardrobe, wherever the dark dominates.

Identify your space with items that stimulate you,
and remove everything that doesn't. What you loved yesterday, you may
dislike today. Your life will flow much more smoothly and surprisingly,
new things will come to you.

If you need change in your life
give away something that you really love, or need, so that unexpected
happenings have room to enter your life. Gifts given away; many gifts
received.

SURROUNDINGS
THE ENVIRONMENT

On a warm, spring April day, one morn
A little bitty seed of a tree was born, in the garden.
With all the warmth of the land it grew
Loved by the rain and the soft warm dew, in the garden.
As it reached for the sky, from a power within,
Its soul cried out and its beauty began.
Love came through from the earth below
And its energy was the power to grow, in the garden.
Just look around, and you will see
All the love coming from this tall green tree, in the garden.
Every morning, as you begin your day
First, look to nature to show you the way.
Does it look grand, strong, and bold?
This means your way will be the path of gold.
If the wind and water and plants seem down,
Don't make plans or decisions right now.
Its nature's way of reflecting your day
So keep this in mind, it's our secret, we say.

Feng Shui is an example
of a practical ancient art which can secure prosperity, respect, good fortune and creativity. Therefore, let it be known that the entrance to any
building should be in clear view; a vision of beauty to encourage good,
positive energy to enter.

Feng Shui must reflect your personal taste,
as the design layout of your building is your energy path which the
ancient masters mapped from the mysterious earth forces. We are
affected by our environment. Pay attention to your intuition, the perfect
balance of Yin and Yang; it is the small voice that speaks to you from
within, known as *formless intelligence.*

Yin and Yang forces run through the earth.
Our bodies (chakra) and our buildings must be acknowledged and kept
in balance so not to be damaged or weakened.

Birth-year energy
According to your birth year, you are identified as an East or West person. The most prosperous building for an East person is one in which
the entry door faces north or south. A West person's prosperous building is one in which the entry door faces southwest or northeast.

HOUSE ENERGY

There are many confusing aspects of charting the energy of the home. It carries its own energy from its creators and its location, but people carry their energy from the year in which they were born. According to Pa Kua energy charts, a person will have East energy if the last number of his-her birth year is 0, 1, 3, 4, and 9. If the birth year ends with 2, 5, 6, 7 or 8 he-she is a West person.

The energy of an East building would be indicated by the direction of the main entrance door. If a building faces (from the inside looking out) south, the house *sits* (opposite) north. The house has a north *location* with a south *direction*. It is where a house 'sits', i.e., its location that determines whether it is and East or West building.

An East building *sits* south, southeast, north and east.

A West building *sits* northeast, northwest, west and southwest.

Moving
Apply Feng Shui to buildings you are moving into, so you know the energy will be healthy and suitable to all and not a place where nagging, arguing, and harassment take place. Check its direction and location.

Pa Kua calculations tells a person's auspicious location and direction calculated from the birthdate.

Know the house history
before you move in, and its direction and location (where it sits), as well as why the people before you moved out of the property. Houses have karma and tend to repeat their histories. Buyers beware.

Structure
A building carries a certain energy from all those who built it, lived in it or visited it. Your intuition is a perfect balance of Yin and Yang energy and tells you if it is right for you. Listen, always, to your inner voice.

Exterior improvements increase the supply of beneficial energies
that flow into the building. Your exterior environment and surroundings represent your past, present, and future (in metaphysical terms).
Strong rear support (past), like a hill, is good. The house should not be
overshadowed on the sides. Have an open clear view (future) with the
front being open without obstruction—a clear path.

Beautiful views
are highly nurturing to the occupants (i.e., windows, art, and photogra-
phy).

Exterior warning to the owner.
Act wisely and know if there were any financial difficulties with the
previous owners, so not to carry vertically these misfortunes and hardships.

Exterior knowledge
is to make an effort to know all you can about the history of the lot and
building, and its previous occupants, for any unhappy or damaging incidents and mishaps.

Exterior overhead wires
should not be situated near the front of the building so as not to over-
activate the metal elements of the building. Hydro wires (negative
energy) can do damage when fixed to the front of the house, causing
poor health issues.

Exterior locations
should be observed. Don't be overshadowed by a neighboring large
building as it absorbs the good fortune energy away from you.

Entrance paths to the entry door
should be well lit, as lights act positively, just as flowers do in the daytime.

Exteriors of the building,
Street numbers should be placed vertically or horizontally. Positioning them diagonally is a sign of indecisiveness.

Exterior numbers
must be visible from the road or the incoming energy will know you are hiding something from others. A sense of clarity is reflective of your personality.

Overgrown landscaping prevents new opportunities
from entering your life as the building disappears behind neglected gardens, and diminishes the energy flow.

Exterior landscaping, such as shrubs blocking the entry,
should be removed so prosperous energy enters the building without blockage.

Exterior landscaping with overgrown gardens that block the view
from any window prevents the sun (fire element) from entering the building. The fire element enhances the owner's abundance, and its flow should not be diminished. .

Exterior clearing is accomplished
by removing any obstruction blocking the view or entry path to the main entrance of the building.

Exterior walkways should always be in good order,
without weeds, cracks, or damage, so as not to bring negative and loss energy into the building.

Exterior landscaping should be cautioned
against placement of spiky plants and shrubs. These can damage or change the flow of energy to negative if they are not situated next to round, leafy greenery for balance.

Exterior curb appeal
is damaged by broken fences, gates, steps, weeds, and clutter. These things indicate neglect and weaken the abundant energy around the building.

Take exterior caution
and beware of sharp protruding corners when entering a building. They should be softened with plants. These sharp corners symbolize poison arrows as they take the shape (pointed edge) of an arrowhead tip. These cutting edges reflect bruising of the energy as it passes.

Exterior beauty can be diminished,
just like your good fortune, when the windows are dirty or chipped paint is apparent.

Exterior sidewalks and garden edges
should be manicured and kept trimmed, free of weeds, so that neglect doesn't attract negative energies which could bring sickness into the building.

Exterior repairs
Always repair any broken, damaged, or cracked areas so as to keep illness away. Damaged areas weaken the creativity energy of the occupants.

Exterior drains and eaves troughs
must be free from clutter so the water and debris flow freely. Good drainage makes sure that the energy around the environment flows freely and stays positive.

Exterior entry doors
are best identified separately by painting them an accent color to
enhance their location and attract positive energy. Color is selected
according to the direction in which the door faces.

Exterior entry-door hardware
should operate smoothly without stiffness or damage, and work easily
to make sure any hardships stay out of the building.

Exterior entry-door sound systems
(intercoms, doorbells, etc.) should be repaired if broken or not operating
correctly, so as not to encourage mishaps or accidents, as any damaged,
broken, or cracked items can.

Exterior obstruction should be noted,
such as lamp posts, trees, or any objects directly in front of the entry.
Such vertical items can cut the energy and weaken it upon entering the
building, thereby preventing new friendships.

Exterior details
Nothing should touch, interfere with, or hinder the structure, especially
the roof, so as not to cause anxiety to the occupants.

Buildings that have no yard or property,
or have a steep drop, leave the occupants with no backing and possibly
financially poor. Buildings prosper with the mountain or a high building behind them for support.

Exterior health can be enhanced
by collecting rainwater in glass containers (earth element) which support the water element by enhancing its energy. Collect the rainwater
and let it sit three hours outside in the sun. This light energy actually
helps one's memory when drunk regularly and can also enhance plant
life.

Exterior walkways
Beware of straight lines! Walkways to the entry of the building where energy enters can become destructive and move too fast. Curved entries are recommended to keep the energy prosperous.

Exterior corners can become traps
if left empty and the energy becomes stagnant. Place an attractive item or greenery there for protection.

Exterior help
Undulating mystical movement of energy can be achieved with flags located strategically on the property.

Exterior chimes
should be conducive to the location. Thus metal chimes in the west will bring good fortune, while wood chimes in the east and crystal in the southwest or northeast do not bring harm to the building. Each element has a specific location for prosperity.

The location of the building
is best situated on the inside of a curved road, rather than on the outside bend of the curved road, for its protection.

Exterior location
of a building placed where a roadway is directed right at it, is overpowered by swift moving energy, reducing all sense of calmness.

Exterior enhancement
is created by a wide open space around the front entry enhanced by a life element (greenery).

 Environmental Issues

After a conference in New York City and a house tour at Street of Dreams in Seattle, I could see plainly that the architects of the day were finally aware of the health issues of our buildings, in which synthetics and off-gassing products had created havoc that needed to be brought to the public's attention.

We start our day with plastic toothbrushes and eat food from plastic packaging. We wear clothes containing more man-made fibers than natural fibers. We look through plastic lenses in our glasses and drive plastic vehicles. Will it never end? Petroleum products have created this plastic planet and it is killing us with poor health and disease. You wonder why we are not healthy?

Alternative natural products are needed throughout our home. Let's be aware and read labels and make healthy choices. These chemical-based products are stagnant energy, and prevent the positive flow from entering.

Condo-living has created another worry, for the homeowner has no choice when selecting a lot of the interior finishes. The developers and suppliers have come up with solutions so that wood and tile floorings can now replace vinyls, laminate floorings, and chemically enhanced carpets. We need more wool, hemp, cotton products, and wood or bamboo that will last and be durable and more healthful.

When you enter a building, whether at work or at home, you can feel the difference when there are no open windows to cleanse the air. A group of students living in an enclosed area often complain of sore muscles, sore throats, and headaches. A number of elderly people become ill only months after moving into a newer residence when they have lived in an older home for years. These newer facilities are put together in the shortest time possible and are built with the cheapest products a lot of the time. The negative energy, created by the off-gassing chemicals and synthetics is harmful. Add plants to the space to help cleanse the air.

In Portland, Oregon, my friend Beth inherited some beautiful pieces of furniture from relatives. She placed the wool oriental carpets over the existing synthetic carpets to reduce the effect to a minimum. The real wood furniture and natural-content fabrics in the furniture were what our parents grew up with, and they were a lot healthier, than now. They were not exposed to the fiberboard construction used in products of today or the formaldehyde. Wood was wood, not filled with other things, non-biodegradable chemical products, and excessive resins.

When Beth was updating her place, she had heard that neighbors had found mold when they had renovated. She was lucky and found none. She selected a water-based stain for her new maple bathroom vanity, a granite counter top, and beautiful tiles for her shower surround and heated floor. Her new floor was limestone, and she had her walls constructed out of concrete board instead of drywall before tiling. There are numerous products for this application now. She got rid of the plastic hardware, replacing it with brushed nickel and no more vinyl. She could breathe a little better and the energy felt positive.

Feng Shui is all about the feeling. When the energy can flow and meander throughout the space, it is positive. You actually feel happier.

It is exciting to work or live in new accommodations, but after a few months, you tend to feel a lot more tired than usual. You may suffer anxiety, headaches, or stiffness. These are the interior problems: sick-building syndrome, SBS.

Exterior-curb appeal is an investment that can increase the value of your home, just by enhancing the structure with the right colors. The home is the largest single investment made by 94 percent of North Americans.

Many older homes in Port Hope, Ontario are beautifully displayed with color. Irwin owns a home in this neck of the woods, and was reluctant to select colors on his own because the colors he liked just didn't do the home justice. Since the front entry faced west, we selected a heritage terracotta color. The color on the front door should not be used elsewhere on the structure so that the energy has no difficulty flowing in the right direction, and this strong statement lets everyone else know as well. Garages should blend into the field color of the house, so as not to attract energy which becomes negative. This smaller home sat next to a much larger one, so his exterior design needed to be invigorating for added strength and visibility. The field (house) was a rich camel shade; the windows were ivory with milk chocolate-colored shutters. The trim and fascia boards were also a mixture of the ivory and chocolate colors.

Lots of terracotta planters complemented Irwin's entry, and were filled with a variety of plants, all in one color for continuity. Irwin was pleased. The house even felt happier.

Color is a strong carrier of energy. It not only has to look good, it has to feel good. It should not be fashionable, or too trendy, so as not to appear dated in a few years. It should complement the architecture, structure, and placement.

A Feng Shui house is under the influence of the elements. The wind and the rain will change the exterior and the colors will fade; cracks, breaks, and damage to the structure will appear; plants and shrubs will overgrow their space; more cracks will appear in the walkways, etc. The changing energy of the elements is affected by the movement and vibrations of the planets, just as our bodies and personalities are ever changing. To keep all things in harmony, one must be aware of the environment all the time.

A house filled with negative energy is one showing neglect. You could say that it is no different with our wardrobe. It must be kept up to date so as not to show neglect, and this care affects our inner and outer energy fields.

Good fun schway … says Grannie!

Supportive energy
is achieved when there is a clear space in front of the building, with a
slow-moving winding road (or sidewalk) nearby, and no high-speed
traffic.

Shapes
When a building's shape is not perfectly square or rectangular, landscape the missing corners to create a completed shape. Use bright
monochromatic colors in the missing area: west would be in white,
while south would be in red or pink tones. To complete the missing
shape, you can also identify it with lights to square it up as part of the
structure.

Change of energy
can occur after renovating a building, as the overall shape could have
been altered from an addition. Noted changes in health (east sector)
and relationships (southwest sector) could be effected (i.e., a house that
was originally rectangular becomes L-shaped with a missing corner).

Metal wind chimes
can diminish ones financial resources if located in the southeast. Consider wood or black colored chimes.

Garage locations can be damaging,
especially if located in the wealth area of the home (southeast). Make
sure the garage is kept in immaculate condition and always clean out
unwanted items and garbage, weekly.

Mailboxes are usually a metal item.
Enhance them with prosperity, such as gold lettering, to attract good
fortune.

Occupants of buildings that lack a strong foundation
could find themselves losing money by not being totally grounded.

Garden areas
A bird bath invites the flow of positive energy if located in the north, east, or southeast sector, and increases prosperity.

Protective energy
to a building can be achieved with plantings around the back and sides providing a protective entrance.

Health
Daily contact with nature cleanses the soul. Care for your garden.

Health
Add a health element to the garden with herbs and food in the east sector.

The five elements,
fire, water, wood, metal, and earth, should always be contained in the landscape design, either with color or with shapes. This balance produces harmony and will enhance a sense of well-being for the occupants.

Earth elements
Statues, rocks, and stone items are placed in the southwest and northeast sectors of the garden.

Harmonize the energy
with sound in the garden; but take care lest chimes become annoying and cause anxiety.

Water elements
such as ponds, fountains, and streams can destroy personal growth and achievements when situated in the south sector of the yard or garden. Keep them to the north.

Cleansing the garden makes room for abundance
Weeds, twigs, branches, and dead blossoms are to be removed regularly, so that relationships in work and at home stay nourished and strong.

Increased opportunities come to a building with well-defined walkways, landings, steps, decks, and patios, which are constructed out of natural elements.

Yard care
has no room for broken pots, tools (Feng Shui identifies them as weapons), debris, dirty steps or patios, damaged furniture, chipped paint, cracked pavement, and walkways. All these deplete the growth energy needed for a harmonized environment and abundance.

Yard care
Leaves should be raked and eaves troughs cleaned out, so things run smoothly and make room for new growth. New energy can correct the environment.

Form school is a type of Feng Shui
that teaches houses built on hills, where the land slopes away, could experience a draining of wealth (loss of needed positive energy) for the occupants.

Beware of Feng Shui knockoffs.
Follow the traditional ancient ways: use a compass, with Career sector always in the north section; use Pa Kua identifying your four best prosperity locations; and always use a compass.

Creative Spaces

Boys and their hot-engine toys!

The North American West Coast has had a strong passion for hot rods since the 1950s. An old car was not just a means of transportation, but it was the dream of the collector to find that first car he owned. There are those who own dozens and those who worship only one. Their passion is always the same. A detailed eye doesn't miss a scratch, rim, taillight, knob, or trunk handle, let alone the uniqueness of how it sits.

These boys can discuss a particular part for an hour or a new component for an afternoon. Day after day, their conversations are endless. Their high energy is unbelievably in harmony. They can finish each others' sentences regarding an engine detail before it is ever spoken.

The boys gather regularly: Jim, Vern, Ken, Larry, Dan, Bob, Ron, not to mention Murray, Al, Gord, Jack, Don, Andy, John, and Cam. There's a new roadster in town and everyone is interested. The comradeship is amazing.

The buildings where these vehicles are created are for the most part totally positive energy and carry all the five elements—a space filled with a guy's heart and soul. The art, love, and inspiration that go into these colorful, shiny treasures are from deep within the heart. I have visited many garages. The law of attraction lingers over the space as one tool is lost and another found, only to be put away at the end of the day. Their design details arise from moments of hesitation, allowing their intuition unlimited expression. Not many of these hot rods are ever duplicated because of this focus to create yet another unique feature.

The millennium has brought the Rat Rod roadster from the fifties back to popularity, as the "real" street rod encouraged a new wave of creativity; another reason to have two hot rods in the garage.

The boys take numerous road trips that also run in harmony. There is never a moment when one downfall or faulty part is not attended to by the whole. A trip is almost never without mishaps, but always a wonderful encounter or new friendship develops from the experience.

The mystical movement of energy is ever present, whether in the garage or on the road. This is an art form on a large scale where creative detailing of each hot rod is of a magnitude like no other. From California to British Columbia, thousands of vehicles display themselves at car shows where many, many thousands of spectators view these amazing pieces of art as they gracefully rumble into position. An overwhelming sense of harmony flows through the environment as a collective audience from children to grandparents enjoy their craft, but never to touch, as the boys embark on spotting yet another new skill, detail, or inspiration.

Never visit the boys' humble abode while they are working. One question could lead to a history of car stories. Their buildings' walls are covered with years of mementos and dreams from when they were teenagers. And, the personality of a "car guy" is one thing when with the boys, and yet quite another when with others; let me tell you.

It all has to do with the creative energy that flows among this brotherhood, as they tenderly caress the fender of their vehicle as if it were a woman, contemplating yet another dream.

Good fun schway ... says Grannie!

ELEMENTS

Environmental energy can be altered

by temperature, lighting, scent, color, and shapes.

Earth's energy field changes yearly.

You carry the earth's energy of your birth year with you all your life. The year 1948 was a Yang Earth energy year; the year 1960 was a Yang Metal energy year; the year 1973 was a Yin Water energy year; the year 1985 was a Yin Wood energy year. What is the energy of the earth that you carry?

All years ending in an *odd* number carry *Yin energy*;
and all years ending in an *even* number carry *Yang energy*.
Years ending in 0 or 1 carry *metal* energy;
years ending in 2 or 3 carry *water* energy;
years ending in 4 or 5 carry *wood* energy; and
years ending in 6 and 7 carry *fire* energy.
The flow of *earth* element energy is for years ending in 8 and 9.
Babies born in 2008 carry *Yang earth* energy throughout their life.

Feng Shui is the use of natural products, earth's energy elements.

The five elements:

Water	enhances wood	drowns out fire
Wood	enhances fire	dominates earth
Fire	creates earth	melts metal
Earth	produces metal	dams water
Metal	holds water	cuts wood

Example:

When a person carries the energy of Yang Metal (i.e., 1980), it means that the element metal energy resonates an electromagnetic field similar to the items represented by metal characteristics, which can enhance the positive energy field.

Metal is represented by:

the colors ... white, grey, and pastels;
the shapes ... round and oval;
the items ... brass, silver, gold chains, jewelry, watches, precious metals, nails, chimes, pins, and many more such items.

Elements

Enhance

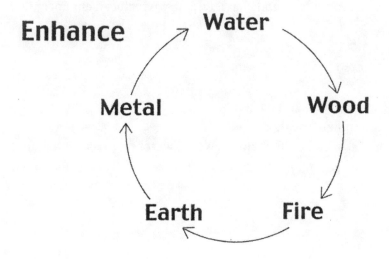

Control

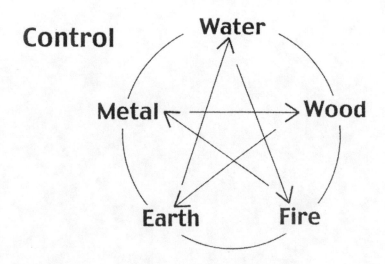

Each compass designation (sector) of a building carries an Element energy.

North	Water	enhanced by (Metal)
Northeast	Earth	enhanced by (Fire)
East	Wood	enhanced by (Water)
Southeast	Wood	enhanced by (Water)
South	Fire	enhanced by (Wood)
Southwest	Earth	enhanced by (Fire)
West	Metal	enhanced by (Earth)
Northwest	Metal	enhanced by (Earth)

Each compass designation (sector) of a building carries an Aspiration energy.

North	Career * Journey
Northeast	Knowledge
East	Health * Family
Southeast	Wealth * Abundance
South	Recognition
Southwest	Relationships
West	Creativity * Children
Northwest	Travel * Friendship

Each compass designation (sector) of a building carries a Color energy.

North	black—blue
Northeast	yellow—brown
East	teal—green
Southeast	green
South	red
Southwest	brown—yellow
West	grey—white
Northwest	pastel—grey

Each compass designation (sector) of a building carries a Shape energy.

North	irregular zig-zag
Northeast	square—rectangle
East	vertical
Southeast	stripe—column
South	diamond—triangle
Southwest	rectangle—square
West	round—oval
Northwest	oval—round

Each compass designation (sector) carries a number energy.

North	one
Northeast	eight
East	three
Southeast	four
South	nine
Southwest	two
West	seven
Northwest	six
Center	five

From the ancient magic square, all numbers placed on a nine-square grid total fifteen, vertically, horizontally, and diagonally. South is located at the top-center square location.

SOUTH

Wood **4** Green	Fire **9** Red	Earth **2** Yellow
Wood **3** Green	Earth **5** Yellow	Metal **7** White/Metallic
Earth **8** Yellow	Water **1** Black/Dark Blue	Metal **6** White/Metallic

Insight "Energy"

Found in nature and the environment through colors and numbers.

Color/Number	Positive	Negative
Black	protection, new birth	sacrifice, secretiveness
Grey	initiation	imbalance
White	purity, truth	overextended, scattered
Violet	alchemy, spirit	obsession, misunderstood
Blue	happiness, truth	depression, loneliness
Brown	new growth	lack of discrimination
Green	healing, abundance	greed, miserly
Yellow	inspiration	over-criticalness
Orange	creativity, joy	agitation, worries
Red	sex, strength	anger, impulse

Color/Number	Positive	Negative
one	beginnings	arrogance
two	dreams, cooperation	meddling
three	creativity, new birth	gossip, moody
four	patience	stubborn
five	versatile, change	overindulgent
six	family, home	worrisome, jealous
seven	truth, wisdom	critical, faithless
eight	power, money	greedy, authoritarian
nine	understanding	gullible, hypersensitive

Each person carries the Element energy of their birth year. See, for example, the chart below for a male born in 1967. (Feng Shui *I Ching* calculations for each person's birthdate produces energy information.) Birthdates give you a Pa Kua number identifying your four auspicious positive and four negative locations.

Yin Fire energy of the earth was during 1967 year:

Wood would be like a parent *enhancement* energy when added.

Water would be like a grandparents *control* energy when added.

Earth would be like the child, which fire *produces* when added.

Metal would be the *weakening* energy when added.

(Follow the arrows in the Element enhancement-control cycle drawing.)

Yin Fire	environmental energy (outer)
West	energy person or building
Sheep	*zodiac* energy animal
Diamond	pointed *shape* energy
Reds	*color* energy
# 6	Pa Kua energy *number*
Northwest	good luck *location* and
Yang Earth	*natal* energy (inner)

Best Locations and directions to face are: West, Southwest, Northeast and Northwest.

Could there be over fifty thousand combinations of the above, depending on each individual's birthdate? (Combinations of twelve yearly zodiac animals times five elements times two yin-yang times ten Pa Kua compass/number locations times two east/west times two male/female times twelve monthly astrological signs, not to mention prosperous numbers, colors, best directions/locations, etc.)

These (above) particulars let you know what you should incorporate into your life when a correction is needed, for harmony, balance, and well-being. They are all calculated from your birthdate.

Fire elements
would be items with a pyramid, diamond, or triangle shape; flame patterns; candles; lights; skylights; fireplaces; barbeques; and colors of red, pink, terracotta, and burgundy. Bright lights on dimmer switches keep the energy controlled, especially in entrances, dining areas, study areas, and dark hallways for safety and clarity.

Earth elements
would include pottery, ceramic, china, crystal, granite, marble, slate, stone, brick, gemstones, garden art; mountain landscapes; items that are square or rectangle; and colors of yellows, brown, and beige.

Water elements
are irregular shapes; colors that are deep and dark, black; and items such as fountains, shells, fish, water, and ocean landscapes.

Metal elements
are shapes that are oval or round; colors of pastels, gray, and white; and items of silver, gold, iron, copper, brass, and metallic.

Wood elements
are items vertical in shape (stripes); green, aqua, or teal in color; botanical items, rattan, hemp, cotton, and floral fabrics; plants; organic items; furniture; natural fiber carpets; art items; and drapery panels.

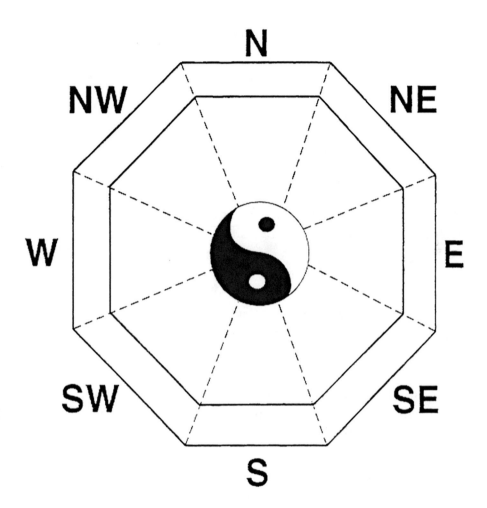

Each person, based on their personal energy charts calculated from their birth year, is either a West or an East person. These calculations also indicate a person's four most prosperous locations for working, eating, and sleeping, as well at their best direction to face. These are your personal Pa Kua calculations.

Each building carries the energy
of the direction in which the front door faces.

Each building is either an East or West building
depending on the location where it sits.

Natural elements carry the most positive flow
of energy; they are very prosperous and healthy to the environment. Wood or tile floors are superior to synthetics, laminates, vinyls, carpeting, etc., due to the latter's volatile chemicals and off-gassing.

Wood elements
can be positive energy in the southeast wealth sector when using striped wall coverings; green or teal-colored paints; and fabrics or natural wood furnishings that activate positive elements.

Feng Shui energy change
is accomplished through colors, shapes, or an element item (e.g., fire equals lamp) which can actually introduce significant changes.

Feng Shui
lists seven aspects for every room which include: life + light + stillness + sound + movement + color + meandering path = harmony.

Remedies for balance of energy in a room.

life	plant
sound	music or clock
stillness	statue or vase
color	art or wallpaper
movement	patterned fabric, drapery
light	lamps, windows

meandering energy paths (no straight lines)

Elements
Limestone is an excellent source of earth to be placed in west entries or rooms.

Elements
China or pottery placed near a water element (artwork or fountain) in the north sector can bring about mishaps and problems within the career.

Design Elements
Consider all seven design elements within the interior for corrections, which would include the floor + walls + windows + lighting + furnishings + color + placement = harmony and balance.

Enhancement and Control Element Remedies

A very confusing part of the Feng Shui exercises is the energy charts. Each person in the family has his-her own specific energy information, and this information is carried with you all the years of your life. If you are an East person with prosperous locations of south, east, north, and southeast, and you are spending a million dollars or more on a property, it would be wise to see that its energy is compatible with yours. Everyone has at one time or another found certain places not to their liking. Your inner sense tells you, and you want to leave before taking a complete look at the premise. This knowing is a reaction or warning against negative energy that you are feeling.

There are times when you feel uncomfortable around certain people and don't want to be working or playing with them, even though you have not really met them or worked with them before. Your energies are not blending, so to speak. They might carry metal energy, and you carry wood energy—and metal cuts or controls wood, so your instinct is saying that this is not a good energy field to be around.

The mystical movement of energy works with you, if you are focused and aware of its warnings. Even if a house is carrying East energy and you are a West person, there are always corrections that can be applied through the realignment of natural elements to enhance the prosperity of the building to suit you. It is a balancing of Yin and Yang principals that put the environment in harmony. You may have visited a location and had a really good feeling about it. It wasn't your taste in decoration, but it just felt good. Some restaurants can give you that feeling.

Exercise.

One of the best ways to find out if you are living in your best energy field is to analyze in detail the room where you spend the most time.

To do this you need a compass to find out its location within the building. If you are an East person, and the room is located in the northwest, you would probably be best sitting in the north or south sectors which are good-energy areas for you. You may want to face east or southeast when working or watching TV. Moving yourself into new positions when things are out of sorts will change the energy flow (within the room) around you. Always change the energy when things aren't going your way. Drive to work by a different route. Sleep on the opposite side of the bed. Sit in another chair. Enter the building from another entrance than the usual one.

You can carry your birth year energy with you, perhaps on a keychain for good fortune. If you are a Yin Wood, perhaps a piece of wood with a whale (fish) on it as water; if you carry the energy of Yang Metal, perhaps a round metal shape with a gemstone in it, etc .

There are people, places, rooms, buildings, and items that we feel comfortable in and around. This is because you are situated in your positive energy field that is compatible with your birth year energy that you carry with you all your life. You know if it is good or bad for you from your intuition and the way you perform. Attention to detail is recommended to keep yourself healthy, creatively inspired, and in good relationships.

Good fun schway ... says Grannie!

Locations
Beware of the element wood which controls or damages earth (which is representative of relationships) in the southwest. Relocate any greenery items out of this area of a room so as not to dominate and weaken the energy.

Locations
Electronics are metal items and weaken one's health when placed in the east, which is the wood element location. Consider a new location for these items and strengthen the family and health area with a water element or the color black.

Locations
White is the energy color for the element metal and should have limited use in the east area so it isn't a weakening factor to the health of the occupants.

Locations
Water-enhancing elements are located in the north representing the career aspiration for abundance and achievements.

Locations
Personal recognition: The south sector of a room should be free of any black objects near lamps or windows so not to weaken ones goals.

Color
Too many dark Yin colors, such as black, brown, and navy, can create a depressed state psychologically and need to be balanced with Yang light colors for a state of harmony. Add a little punch to your wardrobe if you tend to wear a lot of dark colors.

Color

Balance is accomplished by using both warm and cool colors in the same palate.

Fun with Travel

There are numerous ways to have *fun schway* in everyday life. It wasn't that long ago that Kym, a close friend of my daughter's, was interested in traveling, but she was always having some kind of mishap.

She had traveled to England and worked briefly as a nanny, but had to return due to illness. Another trip took her to Spain, and no sooner did she arrive, then she returned back to the west coast. It didn't seem to matter where she went, something always came up to ruin her trip or experience. We chatted about it on numerous occasions and I suggested we should try something to attract some good fortune.

Kym was living in a small apartment where she studied, lived, and slept all in one room. It was a pretty tight place, to say the least.

We spent some time together and I prepared her energy charts based on her birth year. They indicated that she carried the energy of Yang Metal, and she was an East person. I did a compass reading on her apartment finding it was a West house (so to speak). We needed to do some corrections.

With an enlightened, fun attitude, I had Kym restructure her tiny space. It was in need of a big clean-up. Everything had to be reorganized. Lots of books and papers from school years past had to be removed and stored elsewhere. The old material that wasn't required for her current semester had to go. She was also applying to different universities and anticipating a possible move, giving her more reason to clear out her things. Her tiny closet would then provide more space for her and every inch was counted.

With little income other than her twenty hours a week working at the Gap, Kym put together some unique shelving units that covered a whole wall. The room would be painted a soft olive green. Her daybed needed to blend into the color of the wall, so as not to be too visible. The coverlet she found matched perfectly. This helped reduce the size of the bed by camouflaging it into the background, thereby creating more visual space. The shelves also had to blend into the wall, and therefore were also painted out. Numerous large wicker baskets were stacked for needed storage. A tiny drop-leaf table was to be painted white, as were the two stools. Large white pillows for the daybed were added. Nothing went on the walls except a very large bulletin board (cork board) for all her paper clutter that would now be contained and controlled by her. Kym needed to have the head of her daybed face one of her four best directions for sleeping, and being an East person, the room only allowed for one spot that was free of doors or windows. We placed it so her head would face north. She felt comfortable with that.

We sat with a bottle of wine and discussed our next steps. Out came the compass and note paper. It was beginning to feel Zen.

The aspiration Travel is located in the northwest sector (of the compass). And, Kym needed extra money for her trip, so she needed to look for some in the Wealth sector which is the southeast section of the room. The small room needed to be as empty as we could possibly make it because we needed the incoming energy to be attracted to these particular sectors for enhancement.

After plotting her room onto a plan, which we identified by compass directions, we learned that the entry door to her place was in the Travel sector. The northeast sector carries the energy of metal. It was decided to search out a collage of photos and frame them onto a board, artistically. They would identify her travel. Photos of airplanes, travel locations, good weather, etc., were all gathered and applied onto a white (metal color) board and framed in silver metal.

The only place we could hang this was on the wall behind the entry door. Under her collection of pictures, I placed her empty suitcase (which happened to be gray, which is a metal color) with her affirmation written out and placed inside. She identified in detail her desires.

After that, we located the Wealth sector of the room. It was situated where she had placed her long storage-shelf unit. These had been organized with baskets, books, CDs, photos, etc. By leaving a clear section open for a grouping of plants, she placed some affordable violets. The Wealth sector carries the energy of wood and the number 4, so the plants would enhance the area. I wanted her to place four toonies (two-dollar coins) into or under the plants (the idea being to encourage growth when wrapped in red silk). We located a small crystal-clear vase and filled it with distilled water. Kym had received it as a gift and she set it in between the plants to reinforce their growth as water feeds wood.

Everything appeared better. She was pleased with her new space and new look, and even felt happier studying and living there.

Several weeks passed before I had a call from Kym. She was struggling with her exams, work, and a relationship gone sour. We were going to meet for coffee (actually green tea) the following week. By the time we met, she appeared in good spirits.

The ever-changing energy that had come into her life was big, she explained. When it had settled, the exams had gone very well and she also received a small raise from her work. She didn't say anything about the relationship, so I thought better not to mention it. Kym was in good spirits now. She had been accepted at a university in Quebec and was getting ready for a new venture in Montreal.

Just days before she was to fly east, Kym received an unexpected call from friends who wanted her to travel south to the Cayman Islands with them. No expenses. It wasn't her dream trip to the Canary Islands, but it ended up being better than she could have ever dreamed.

Kym graduated from McGill University and went on to get a Masters degree in women's studies; she was accepted for her PhD study at the University of Toronto at the age of twenty-four.

She still loves to travel, keeping her toonie in her violets in the southeast sector of her room.

Good fun schway … says Grannie!

Color
Blues should be limited in areas of boardrooms and bedrooms because it is a water representation and can have a draining effect on the space. It can be combined with earth yellow or beige to control its moving effects. (Earth dams water.)

Shapes
Square or rectangle shapes are prosperous when located in the northeast or southwest (earth representations) when selecting doors, windows, tables, planters, patios, mirrors, art, carpets, etc.

Shapes
Oval or round shapes are prosperous when located in the west area of a room when used as tables, mirrors, art, rugs, planters, plates, or in fabric prints.

Shift in energy
Consider round mirrors in the west; square mirrors in the southwest; and vertical mirrors in the east.

Not coping well with life's changes
can be from too much black (water element) as one seeks the dark—winter. Add touches of red (fire) or white (metal) to the space or your wardrobe where the dark dominates.

Fear
is cleansed with metal or water (black or white) corrections in areas such as the bladder, kidneys, ears, bones, head, and hair.

Anger
is cleansed (wood or water) with greens or blues in areas such as the nails, eyes, liver, and gallbladder.

Joy
is enhanced (fire or wood) with red or greens in areas such as the heart
and intestines.

Negative bad luck energies happen
when items of fire or earth elements are in the north sector.

Negative bad luck energies happen
when items of water or metal elements are in the south sector.

Negative bad luck energies happen
when items of fire and wood elements are in the west sector.

Negative bad luck energies happen
when items of earth or metal elements are in the east section.

AWARENESS

Multitasking

is the ability to fill up time and space

so that you don't.

Time becomes rigid in routine.

Be conscious of all things you do.

An East building
is considered to *sit* (location) in east energy in the south, north, east and southeast. This means that the front entry door of the building faces the direction of north, south, west, or northwest as the location is the opposite side of the facing direction. The most prosperous East building is when the facing direction of the entry is either north or south (when looking from the inside out) because this is the only direction and location combination that carry east energy for both facing and sitting.

A West building
is considered to sit (location) in west energy in the west, southwest, northwest and northeast. This means the front entry door faces the opposite direction, east, northeast, southeast and southwest. The most prosperous West building is one where the facing direction of the entry is either northwest or northeast (when looking from the inside out) because this is the only direction and location combination that carry west energy for both facing and sitting.

Interior appearance has a hidden agenda.
Dust mirrors, clean windows, and clean all glass surfaces regularly to keep away all impurities.

Interior life elements
Greenery should be cared for. Always remove dead leaves and blossoms; this is like removing old baggage from our lives, which drags us down.

Interior walk-through the premises regularly,
and note any damage, wear, or required repairs and touch-ups. As soon as they are identified, these damages should be attended to in order to prevent illness from entering.

Interior corners should not be left empty
as the energy can become trapped and stagnant. This can cause forgetfulness for the occupants. Place a loved item or greenery in the area.

Interior hallways are a concern.
Reduce fast-flowing energy within long corridors or hallways to maintain balance within the building with the placement of plants, furniture, moldings, sconces, art, or other items.

Interior observation
Make note that negative rooms are wet rooms (i.e., bathrooms, kitchens, and laundry rooms).

Holding onto the past
Remove all unwanted presents or gifts and hand-me-downs that are not totally loved, no matter where they came from. They hold energy that vibrates and takes up space where it is better to have nothing, leaving room for special items.

Overhead awareness
of restrictions, such as hanging objects, that can gather dust, restrict energy flow, and encourage stagnation, not to mention forgetfulness.

Neglect
Do not neglect any space in the building. All spaces must be nurtured, avoiding cold, junk, and neglected areas that discourage productivity and progress.

Cleansing
Remove negative energies from a room after an argument, unwanted guests, sickness, quarrels, or romantic breakups, by lighting a candle, playing favorite music, and doing a thorough cleansing of the space.

Interior entry is the location where the building inhales the energy at its front entry; therefore it should be cleansed and enhanced with a flowing flowering plant or floral bouquet for beauty. This location should never face trash, polluted waters, or anything damaged or broken.

Interior entry is a place of welcoming
and should be free from clutter so the positive energy can circulate freely. Place something special in this space.

Entry doors are not to face a staircase,
especially if the stairs are split (level) going both up and down, which is the worst configuration creating some complications for all those living in the building. This is an area where you hang wind chimes between the doorway and the stairs.

Interior entry should never have a mirror
(reflective surface) opposite the entry door as it deflects the incoming positive energy back out, which can add difficulties to the building's prosperity.

Interior entry should be free from obstruction;
especially behind the entry door so not to bring hardships into the welcoming area of the building.

Interior entry needs movement to encourage the energy,
and this is a very good location for wall coverings that have movement in their patterns.

Interior entry area should be free from bathrooms,
which can flush the incoming positive energy down the drain. Always have the door closed.

Interior entry area should be free of windows
located opposite the entry door to the building, as the energy will flow
in and out of the building quickly leaving the building without any
prosperity.

Improvement in Health

An extremely hot, summer day in August comes to mind when discussing health issues. One of my contacts was Ray, owner of a family business. He was a very active individual with a great personality. I couldn't believe my ears when I visited his shop to find out from staff that he was no longer coming in due to poor health. In fact, it was a lot worse than poor health.

I was to find out that he not only had cancer, open heart surgery, and several angina attacks, but had experienced TIAs numerous times. (Transient Ischemic Attack or small strokes) Never had I heard about these conditions. I contacted his daughter, who was a client, and made inquiries, and said I would like to speak to him as soon as he was able.

His situation remained on my mind during the following weeks. I needed to place an order, so again, I went into the shop. Dorothy, Ray's wife, was working that particular Tuesday. We had a brief chat about my order for custom hardware. She inquired about some upcoming Feng Shui seminars. I said I would email her some information, then proceeded to make inquiries about Ray. We decided we would all meet for lunch the following week.

It was early September now and we met late one morning at a restaurant on the Selkirk waterfront. We ordered beverages and took some time before looking at the menu. I was quick to inquire about all their mishaps over the last year.

Ray explained to me in detail the complications he experienced. It was just mind-boggling to hear it all, and to see how his health had deteriorated. I suggested that maybe we could look at their home together and see if there were any corrections that could be made to help with a quicker recovery. They were ready to look into any new solution. We enjoyed our lunch together and made plans to meet the following day. I hadn't realized that their accommodations were above their shop. This was a renovation they had done about eighteen months before.

I arrived in the early afternoon. We did a quick walk-through of the apartment. I learned that he had started to fail around the time of the renovations. Before they had moved onto the premises, they were both reasonably well. I applied the compass to the entry, learning that the unit was considered a West house because the entry door faced northeast, therefore the house sat in a westerly location, being southwest.

According to the energy charts of Ray, he was an East person. Not a great beginning. We walked to where the bedroom was situated. At first glance, it was obvious we could apply some realignment to encourage a healthier space for Ray.

The most important issue in health correction is to allow as much positive energy as possible to reach the people sleeping in the room. In this particular case, the bedroom location in the unit was in the northeast sector (not great for Ray). Negative energy was apparent all through the room. The head of the bed was on the west wall (his Total Loss, known as Chueh Ming location). The bed was covered with a decorative canopy which had to go in order to open up the space, to allow more healing energy to reach him. It is essential that nothing be overhead.

There were numerous knickknacks along a ledge behind the bed which had to be cleared off, as less is best. Artwork located on the wall behind the headboard had to be removed so as not to interfere with the flow of positive energy. There were two corner walls (sharp edges) protruding directly at him as he lay in bed. This is a noted poison arrow. The windows were over-decorated and had to be scaled down to allow more fire (sun) energy into the room.

A twelve-foot wall of sliding mirror doors (which is a real no-no in the bedroom) had to be attended to. They represent water energy (reflective surface) and too much movement, constantly activating the energy when it needs to be meandering and calm. This is not a healing element. By the look on his face, he appeared relieved to think we might be able to encourage a better space for him. Even Dorothy was encouraged.

The following day, we immediately began to clear out the room removing excess furnishings and items that could be placed elsewhere or be removed completely. We relocated the bed so he no longer faced the bathroom door, and would now be in one of his best locations according to his energy chart, and have a commanding view of the entry door to the bedroom.

Both Dorothy and Ray agreed to apply wall coverings onto the mirrored doors. A new paint color was recommended in a suede finish with less drama, in a more neutral, healing shade. The flowered bedding (wood element) would be replaced with a less-patterned fabric. It would be in a color that blended into the wall color so as not to add any business to the room, and then the bed would visually fade into the wall color to keep the space as calm as possible. The bathroom door was to be kept closed at all times, all drains plugged, and the toilet seat kept down, so not to lose healthy, positive energy down the drains.

Several days later, we finished. I made some recommendations for the rest of the unit. I explained it was not the best energy field for the bedroom to be located over the garage. (This is something to remember.) I also recommended he change the position of his seating at the dining table and change the location of the TV so he would be facing a healthier direction and would sit in one of his more prosperous locations. I knew the change in energy flow would benefit him.

It was early December when I received a message to pick up some products at Ray's shop. I ventured over to find Ray back at work. I was impressed that he looked so good. He couldn't believe how energetic he felt. He explained that all the medications he had been on finally felt like they were working and his recovery was so much better. Good news to hear that by removing the negative energy from his environment, he had begun to receive a more positive flow. He felt the difference.

Now, I told him … clean up your desk! He laughed. But, he did it because he knew that when the outward energy of his environment was tended to, then his inward healing could begin. Another good sign was when he enlisted into yoga-breathing exercises, reducing a stressful life-style.

Good fun schway ... says Grannie!

Harmful plants
are prickly plants (cactus) or have spiky leaves. Keep these out of the
dining area and always next to round leaf plants.

Relationships
Two natural crystals located side by side add to the love luck in the
southwest sector.

Lack of inspiration
Fireplaces are a fire element and the color red and candle groupings as
well as large windows on the west wall. These will decrease or stagnate
the aspiration Creativity and Children which is located in the West sector of the room.

Correct staircases
are located facing the entry door, as the strong downward flowing
energy needs to slowdown, and this is accomplished by placing a small
mirror at the bottom of the stairs to reflect it.

Yin and Yang balance
Hard and soft flooring; warm and cool colors, high and low ceilings,
dark and light furniture are the Yin and Yang of the interior and therefore must harmonize.

Protective energy can be achieved
by camouflaging a poor window view with a beautiful covering, which
still provides the needed light.

Safety
Lower your stress level. Note any loose, sliding carpets causing danger-
ous space when sloppy.

Caution
Beware of overhead fans. Have them disappear into the color of the ceiling and go unseen; blend out of sight so not to drain positive, prosperous energy.

Wall groupings can have too many items
which depict confusion and signal imbalance of energy, affecting friendships and relationships. Thoughts and focus can become weakened by obstacles, getting in the way.

Good communication
and space planning allows for an eight-foot maximum space between cross seating distance for a balanced flow that is harmonized (knee to knee when sitting).

Tiredness and laziness
can be a sign of stagnant energy. Clear off the window sills; remove blockage that hinders light coming into the space and open the window.

Interior lighting must be in working order at all times.
Make sure there are no burnt-out bulbs, broken switches, or cracks. Damages should be repaired as lights are a fire element and need power to boost the energy forward.

Colorful fruit bowls
situated on tables are an excellent life element expressing abundant energy, only to attract more.

Electronic devices
such as televisions and stereos represent the element metal, and therefore should not be placed in the east area of a room (wood). Metal cuts wood (controls it) so that the room will resonate with negative energy.

Universal Flow and Electromagnetic Fields

Multitasking! This became the jargon of the eighties supermoms, or stay-at-home dads in the nineties. But, I had a few clients that just could not cope with it all.

When it came time to visit their home, it was like their last cry for help. It was plain to see that the last twenty-five years of this high-pace lifestyle in the Western world had produced a hectic homelife for a lot of families. The pace has not slowed at all.

Houses and offices were jam-packed with everyday stuff that never finds a home for itself. Everyone appeared to be taken care of; the meals were made, the kids got to their sports events, school, piano lessons, or whatever else they were involved with, but the stress level of multi-tasking appeared definitely high. It looked like things never got put away; just set aside. Laundry was another story.

No one seemed to have time for a leisurely lunch or dinner, let alone breakfast. The organic foods, counting carbs, and cholesterol-free items just don't matter to a lot of families. Fast food meals were what fit into the time slot between schedules. There was no time. The house actually felt stressed everywhere I looked. But, there was usually one room in order. It was the room that nobody ever went into; just in case someone visited, it appeared organized.

Everyone in the family was talking, and no one was listening. Pets, phones, visitors, were coming and going all at once. Do you know any family like this?

Remember in Europe how everyone had two-hour lunches and the shops actually closed so that conversation, good food, and relaxation were experienced by all? They had a balance of leisure time. But, when our society takes a breather, peoples minds still race with thoughts of so many things they have to do, remember, or not forget, that even quiet times become stressful.

Our environment (outward) reacts similarly to our thoughts (inward). We see what is reflected from our thoughts. Laws of attraction, like attracts like, is the same for our personal space as it is for our inner thoughts. Be careful what you think!

If our surroundings and environment are busy with lots of stuff, then they attract a busy, cluttered mind. A Zen, calm space attracts a clear, productive mind. We are what we see (reflections).

The energy that surrounds you is a reflection of what's inside of you. Negative messiness attracts more complications into your life. So, if any items are broken, then mishaps happen. Less is best and that is one of the reasons why some people seem to be overactive, continually multi-tasking. Just check and see if their environment is full of stuff, especially in cupboards, garages, basements, attics, etc.

I can work with a client and find numerous boxes in their garage or basement. They tell me they have never been opened, but they just keep moving them from house to house. If they don't need to be opened or used every few months, then get rid of the old baggage, and feel less burdened. Boxes full of stuff that's not even wanted, let alone needed, do not need to take up space, precious real estate.

Our negative thoughts attract more negativity and unhappiness because the flow of (positive) energy does not respond to negative words. If you say, "I *don't* want to live like this anymore," the desired (positive) energy reads it as, "I *want* to live like this" so a lot of our wishes never come to pass. Everything you think or say that has negative words in it will be interpreted without those negative words because the positive energy wants to reach you, and therefore will not compute them. Your inner positive energy wants to attract the same. Warning: Be careful not to agree with others when they speak negatively.

You cannot see electricity, or the wind, or music, but you can feel and understand its benefits, knowing it is there. Quantum physics notes that everything vibrates and has motion. There are sounds that our pets hear, but we don't hear. It is the mystical movement of energy that we don't see, but know that it is there. We feel it.

Whenever wrong comes into your life, rethink back to the actual words you said or thought, and then take a look around your environment. It is all interconnected. If the environment is out of harmony, most likely so is your busy mind (which can deprive you of needed sleep).

"Where do we begin?" is the comment heard from many families. Before healing, calm your insides. You will feel a whole lot better when you start with your environment first. If you see and feel harmony, then you will be calmer and so will everyone else within the space.

Begin at the beginning. Be organized. Set schedules for everyone and everything. For positive movement of energy, there has to be space for its movement. Nothing can be in the way, on the floor, on tables, on dressers, or behind entry doors. Think clearly.

Be healthier by being outdoors more. Enjoy nature and let it nurture your soul. Find your own quiet space for half an hour every single day. Breathe deeply three times beforehand when stressed or just go for a walk. This time and space alone will refresh you so decisions will be easier and you will begin to find everything less stressful. You will soon find the need not to multitask. Once the positive energy reaches you, a sense of well-being and calm enters your life. Even a soft color scheme can effect your environment.

We all collect way too much stuff which somehow reflects back on us with way too much thinking (busy mind), and we need to reduce as well as relax. A need for clarity and a need to live a more Zen life can be achieved. It is healthier.

Take two-hour lunches without guilt, as well as good food, conversation, family, and friends. Surround yourself with positive energy flow and don't let anyone drain you of your energy.

Your home and environment are a direct reflection of your inner being. Get help and clean it up. Be organized. Be healthier. You will feel the difference.

Good fun schway ... says Grannie!

Make more empty spaces
which will present themselves as opportunities. Remove throws, pillows, items on table tops, excess art, and accessories, always leaving at least 50 percent of all surfaces empty. This is so that there is ample room for the energy of new opportunities and happiness to enter.

Enhancing the sector
Spiritual knowledge is your inner intuition and the sector is the northeast area. The ancient Vedic science of India (Vaasta) says never be in this location more than a few hours so its energy is always free from obstruction.

Enhancing the sector
Careers can be kick-started when taking the element of the sector (water) and combining it with its enhancing element (metal) side by side. Water elements (fountains, water art, shells, black and navy colors) combined with any metal objects (white and gray colors or round shapes) are placed together in a clear corner of the north sector.

Enhancing the sector
Financial distress can begin to turn around with the wood element (plants, but not overgrown) when situated in the southeast area next to a water element (fountain), in a clear corner so the incoming energy can enhance its vibrations.

Living and family rooms and reception areas
require all five elements, because of the variety of people who enter, to keep the energy in balance and accommodate everyone. These elements must be placed in their specified areas, such as wood elements in the east, water elements in the north, etc.

Interior dining areas or eating space should be separate
from the working kitchen, as a kitchen's negative energy can affect the digestion.

Interior dining or eating spaces can be damaging to health
when located beneath a bathroom (on the floor above) as family
nourishment becomes pressed down by negative energy. Put an up-lite
fixture on the ceiling to control this energy.

Interior dining
is enhanced by placing a mirror opposite the dining table, which is a
symbol of helping double abundance for the occupants.

Interior dining
Artwork should be an expression of abundance, lushness, wealth,
longevity, and good fortune.

Interior dining
Each person at the table should face one of their four auspicious
directions when eating to enhance good health.

Interior dining
The center of the dining table is an earth representation, and can be
enhanced with crystal, ceramic, pottery, and glass, as well as with
candles.

Interior dining
Never eat food from any off-gassing surface, such as plastic, Teflon, or
chemically enhanced surfaces. Throw out all plastic containers,
Styrofoam, etc. They cause poor health.

Interior dining
A table should be enhanced with high-back chairs that are supportive,
while low-back seating leaves the occupant unsupported and vulnerable,
especially when its back is to an open doorway.

Interior dining
Tables that are round or oval are conducive to positive energy and friendly-flowing energy for discussions.

Interior lighting
usually suggests the triangle of three lamps across a room for adequate fire elements.

Lighting (fire elements)
is recommended in tri-lite products for well-lit spaces offering three stages of brightness, so the occupant is always in control of this powerful element.

Furnishings
Round or demilune windows and tables are best placed on a west wall or northwest wall of a building to add creative energies to the home, as well as enhancing the sector of friendships and travel.

Color enhancement needs balance.
Don't be bottom heavy in texture and color, such as dark furniture with no balance of the top. For a sense of harmony consider drapery rods or crown molding.

RELATIONSHIPS

What you see in others,

is your own reflection.

Contemplate what their actions mean to you,

and what they are trying to tell you.

Locations of private rooms
should be located the furthest distance from the front entry.

Avoid inappropriate relationships
that sadden and drain your energy, which resonates in the space around
you wherever you go, attracting mishaps and negative energy.

Feng Shui recommends that when you work,
relax, or sleep, it is always healthier when facing your most prosperous
direction known as Sheng Chi.

Feng Shui recommends removing
electronic items and toys from bedrooms. They interfere with the
earth's electromagnetic field, especially when sleeping.

Best directions
When sleeping with the headboard of a bed facing the most prosperous
direction (one of the four), remember that everyone wakes up refreshed
when they are located in their best location (Sheng Chi).

Sleep
A good strong headboard is always recommended for maximum support and clarity of mind, and good sleep.

Warning not to place any items
on the wall over the head of the bed, as the body needs to attract all the
positive energy it can get while sleeping.

Energy flow in the bedroom is enhanced
when reflective surfaces are removed from the bedroom, especially any
mirrors, as it activates the energy and the bedroom needs to remain
calm.

Don't sit, eat, or sleep under an overhead light fixture (fire element). It subconsciously poses a threat not to mention headaches.

Feng Shui warns of never sitting or sleeping
under overhead beams for any length of time. This has been known to cause unwanted mishaps, lack of creative thought, tiredness, anxiety, and moodiness.

Warning to reduce the number of living plants
in the bedroom, so not to use up needed oxygen. They do assist in absorbing the off-gassing from carpets and other volatile materials and objects.

Feng Shui warns of sleeping beneath a window (fire element)
which can reduce support unless fully covered.

It is wise to have a clear view
of the bedroom door from the bed; always remain in control.

Feng Shui warns of water elements
which are negative in the bedroom and, therefore, en suite bathrooms should always have the door closed.

Bedroom doors should not line up
or face another door across the corridor causing conflicting energy patterns. This can be corrected with a strong up light on the ceiling.

 Communication

There is a magnetism created between two people when they are in balance. It is joyful fun and good times. The principal of attraction when creating harmony happens when emotions and feelings are aroused both mentally and physically.

I carry with me a silver letter *M*, or is it *W*? It all depends on how you look at it. In ancient times, the creation of obelisks, pyramids, and wall art with triangles were plentiful. The upward point designated the male, positive and giving energy, while the inverted triangle was the female, negative and receiving energy. When combined together, they create the five pointed star—identifying the five elements. When encircled, you have the balance of life as shown in the Enhancement and Control Charts.

For me, the letter *W* (with its center upward point) represents the giving-it, but then another would look at this letter to represent the female with its two valleys, the receiving-it; but the *M* for me (with its center valley) is the receiving-it for the feminine energy. It's my Yin and Yang reminder for controlling my emotional energy. Being in harmony.

When a discussion is taking place, there can be a lot of pyramids, lots of giving-it going on, and not a lot of valleys, receiving-it energy; and therefore, we have arguments. There is no balance, so there is no resolution.

There must always be a balance of both energies for the perfect relationship. Great souls know intuitively when to exercise these energies, as the pyramid male energy is considered a temporary submission and distinctively more intellectual, while the valley female energy that receives it is nonresistant with a sense of freedom and essentially spiritual. This acknowledges the impelling power while creating harmony through its wisdom. This combination is the human magnet.

The ancient sage was a person of wisdom who was the choiceless watcher that exercised knowingly, according to the requirements of the situation. You need to observe before you react. Compromise by paying attention to your own magnetic field of emotional energy.

You are able to control your conditions as you come to sense the purpose of what you attract by your vibrating emotions working positively or negatively around you. There is a time and place when the positive (giving-it) energy and a time when the negative (receiving-it) energy works to your advantage. When you are giving instructions, you are in the positive, and when receiving the instructions, you are in the negative. There are times when we need to be the choiceless watcher, and just listen. The observer.

Realigning the romance area of the home is in the southwest sector of the bedroom and depending on the occupant's Energy charts, there are good and bad locations for the bed. It is usually said that the person paying for the household has the bed facing their best direction, then the other person gets to pick which side of the bed is best for them. Compromise creates harmony.

When a breakup or separation has occurred, or an unwanted guest has left, the first thing to do at this time is to get rid of the past energies. That means remove all personal items from bedding to gifts, and then reenergize the room with new paint and realignment of furnishings, if at all possible. A good cleansing of the space can enhance ones magnetic energy field.

New relationships are enhanced with candles (two) and artwork (two). Keep the number of pillows to a minimum on the bed and in twos, or you may be inviting unwanted people or incidents into your relationship. A single pillow may indicate you are satisfied being on your own. Notice if there are any single items in the room, or pictures with only one person.

Dan and Lorraine live in Riverside, California, and have two children. There are lots of ups and downs raising children. Keeping things harmonious around the home does have its problems. The balance of positive (male: giving-it) energy and negative (female:

receiving-it) energy is difficult in the best of times. It is only after a situation happens that they can stand back and analyze who was in what energy field. Clearing the air is like clearing the room. When they get rid of the papers, toys, dishes, clothes, etc., they can actually feel the harmony of the environment resonating with their inner energy, and with their kids' as well. The giver and receiver must listen, and then there is harmony. When there is harmony, there is love, laughter, and kindness.

A good exercise is to actually look back at your day and make note of how many times, in situations at work, home, etc., you were carrying Yang (masculine) or Yin (feminine) energy in the relationships encountered. Were you giving-it or receiving-it? Were you the observer?

Maybe, it is time for you to carry the letter *M* on your keychain, or is it *W*?

Good fun schway ... says Grannie!

Negative energy within the bedroom
can have serious ill effects. Be aware.

Feng Shui warns that staircases should not line up
with a bedroom door causing fast-flowing energy to enter the room.
This space is one that needs to be tranquil and calm, holding the positive energy in place.

Negative energy directed toward the bed
would incorporate any clutter, poison arrows, sharp corners, and any damaged, broken, or cracked items, especially in an L-shaped room.

Negative energy can be created from open bookshelves
which should be covered, just like mirrors at bedtime, as they cause damage, headaches, and mishaps when aimed at the bed.

Bad luck
Clutter in the bedroom can provoke bad luck and missed fortunes. This room is where you spend many hours.

Feng Shui recommends that the bed should be clear
of things tucked beneath it which encourage aches, pains, and difficult times.

Feng Shui recommends never having a bedroom entry door
opposite or across from a window so that the entering energy does not flow directly out. This can cause a loss of energy to the occupant's room and weaken ones creative intuition.

It is wise to remember that the southwest section
of the bedroom is the relationship area of the room and should be enhanced with two crystals, two red candles, or loved photos to strengthen its energy. Never have this space cluttered.

Loss
Be aware of open fireplaces in the bedroom, which can drain (or burn) much of the romance out of the relationship.

Weakening of the relationship
occurs when the bedroom is over-decorated or contains bold colors and patterns.

Good support
Make sure a wall is situated behind the head of the bed. It is not recommended to place the bed across a corner, for such placement causes lack of support and weakens relationships.

Calming colors
are recommended for bedrooms of extrovert children. Such colors won't accelerate the energy flow.

Feng Shui warns to pick up before sleep
as any clutter disrupts sleep, as does anything left on the floor and this negative energy may cause nightmares.

The bedroom is best left for sleeping only,
but if a study area is required, it is best situated in the northeast (Knowledge area) of the room for enhancement. This is an excellent area to hang diplomas, awards, and trophies.

Children's happiness
and sleep patterns can be altered by a negative location. Troubled, unhappy children are usually situated facing the wrong way when sleeping, eating, or studying. Everyone has four prosperous, healthy directions to face based on their Pa Kua energy charts and the other four are negative.

Growing years
Children's rooms that have any electronics drain the positive energy. These devises should be turned off and covered at night, or removed altogether. These items can leave a child lethargic and tired during the day. Merely unplugging them can help save health and the environment.

Babies need to be situated in their healthy location,
with their heads facing their best direction for a peaceful, harmonized flow of energy. The restless child is trying to relocate his-her positive energy field.

Over-stimulated kids
are a consequence of lack of calm, not to mention poor diet. To increase focus, calm the space and create storage for their clutter that is easy for them to utilize; better productivity and marks will be noted.

Feng Shui reminds us that all closets need to be de-cluttered regularly. The rule: If any item is not used in a five-month period, remove it, as its neglect weakens the positive energy. When kids outgrow their toys, create shelving twelve to eighteen inches from the ceiling so they can still see their toys before they are taken away. This should be a slow progression.

Positive energy can be created by having all closet hangers
in the bedroom closets match in color. It is best to have them color coded to the person's birth year energy element (wood-green; metal-white/grey or an actual metal material; water-black or navy etc).

Bedroom locations over garages
the occupants will awake restless and experience constant small problems. This location is better suited for a seldom used guest room, than the master bedroom.

Closet cleanse
If an item has not been used or worn in the past five months, remove it; if an item has not been used in a year, get rid of it. Move on and stop holding onto the past.

Drawers should be cleaned out regularly
so only positive energy enters and leaves as they are opened. Messy lingerie drawers could follow you with negative energy all day and reduce clarity.

Positive energy is enhanced by having everything contained
in the closets placed on shelves or in boxes/baskets Leave nothing lying loose. This shows that you are in control of your 'things' and not the other way around.

Compatible Relationships

In 2003, I visited Hong Kong, a city filled with Feng Shui alignment in its architecture, gardens, and roadways. I was soul-searching for a zodiac calendar with references suitable to a North American culture. This had been an ongoing search for many years and it wasn't until I made this trip that I found the perfect one with the right explanations.

While Hong Kong's nighttime brilliance reflects into its harbor waters with its high energy, towering skyline, and colorful signage, it was devastating to see, as a North American, the daytime view of so many bamboo scaffoldings. At all the high-rise construction sites, hundreds of employees worked without proper hard hats, boots, supports, or tools. The sight of them appearing to dangle over the busy streets below, took my breath away. It was common to hear of deaths every week during the boom construction years. A city without proper building codes is filled with negative energy.

During this time I ventured on a short boat trip with friends to Macao, a magnificent example of mixed Portuguese and Chinese heritage. This mystical yet eerie island was where I finally located the zodiac calendar that I had been searching for. It was in Cathedral Square that I located this treasure, which seemed to jump out from the shelves of a rumpled old bookshop. The faded sheets of the unused tablemats described each animal with the appropriate characteristics I had been searching for. I had read many, many books over the years, yet I could never find the right wording until that moment.

My workshops and seminars include this zodiac calendar and owe their success to its accuracy. Client responses have judged the animal likenesses, summarized below, to be 80 to 95 percent correct. And, I think that is totally good fun schway!

The Ox

The Ox person is regarded as solid and dependable.
Oxen are excellent organizers and systematic in their approach to every task they undertake.
They are not easily influenced by others ideas.
Loyalty is part of their make-up, but if crossed or deceived, they will never forget.
Oxen do not appear to be imaginative, although they are capable of good ideas.
Although not demonstrative or the most exciting people romantically, they are entirely dependable and make devoted parents.
They are people of few words but fine understated gestures.
Oxen are renowned for their patience, but have their limits; once roused, their temper is a sight to behold.

Ox is compatible with snake and rooster.

The Tiger

The tiger is dynamic, impulsive, and lives life to the full.

Tigers often leap into projects without planning, but their natural exuberance will carry them through successfully, unless boredom creeps in and they do not complete the task.

Tigers do not like failure and need to be admired.

If their spirits fall, they require a patient ear to listen until they bounce back again.

They like excitement in their relationships and static situations leave them cold.

Tigers are egotistical.

They can be generous and warm, but will also sometimes show their claws.

Tiger is compatible with horse and dog.

The Rabbit

The rabbit is a born diplomat and cannot bear conflict.

Rabbits can be evasive and will often give the answer they think someone wishes to hear rather than enter into a discussion.

This is not to say they give in easily; the docile cover hides a strong will and self-assurance.

It is difficult to gauge what rabbits are thinking and they can often appear to be constantly daydreaming, though in reality they may be planning their next strategy.

The calmest of the animal signs, rabbits are social creatures up to the point when their space is invaded.

Good communication skills enable rabbits to enjoy the company of others and they are good counsellors.

They prefer to keep away from the limelight where possible and to enjoy the finer things of life.

Rabbit is compatible with goat and pig.

The Dragon

The dragon will launch straight into projects or conversations with a pioneering spirit.

Dragons often fail to notice others trying to keep up, or indeed those plotting behind their backs.

Authority figures, they make their own laws and cannot bear restriction. They prefer to get on with a job themselves and are good at motivating others into action.

They are always available to help others, but their pride makes it difficult for them to accept help in return.

Although they are always at the center of things, they tend to be loners and are prone to stress when life becomes difficult.

Hard-working and generous, dragons are entirely trustworthy and loyal friends.

They enjoy excitement and new situations.

When upset, they can be explosive, but all soon forgotten.

Dragon is compatible with rat and monkey.

The Snake

The snake is a connoisseur of the good things in life.

Inward-looking and self-reliant, they tend to keep their own counsel, dislike relying on others.

They can be ruthless in pursuing their goals.

Although very kind and generous, snakes can be demanding in relationships.

They find it hard to forgive and will never forget a slight.

Never underestimate the patience of a snake, who will wait in the wings until the time is right to strike.

They are elegant and sophisticated and although they are good at making money, they never spend it on trifles.

Only the best is good enough for them.

Very intuitive, snakes can sense the motives of others and can sum up situations accurately.

If crossed, snakes will bite back with deadly accuracy.

They exude an air of mystery, ooze charm, and can be deeply passionate.

Snake is compatible with ox and rooster.

The Horse

The horse is very active.

Horses will work tirelessly until a project is completed, but only if the deadline is their own.

Horses have lightning minds and can sum up people and situations in an instant, sometimes to quickly, and they will move on before seeing the whole picture.

Capable of undertaking several tasks at once, horses are constantly on the move and fond of exercise.

They may exhaust themselves physically and mentally.

Horses are ambitious and confident in their own abilities.

They are not interested in the opinions of others and are adept at side-stepping issues.

They can be impatient and have explosive tempers, although they rarely bear grudges.

Horse is compatible with tiger and dog.

The Goat/Sheep

The goat is emotional and compassionate.

Peace-lovers, goats always behave correctly and they are extremely accommodating to others.

They tend to be shy and vulnerable to criticism.

They worry a lot and appear to be easily put upon, but when they feel strongly about something they will dig their heels in and sulk until they achieve their objectives.

Goats are generally popular and are usually well cared for by others.

They appreciate the finer things in life and are usually lucky.

They find it hard to deal with difficulties and deprecation.

Ardent romantics, goats can obtain their own way by wearing their partners down and turning every occasion to their advantage.

They will do anything to avoid conflict and hate making decisions.

Goat is compatible with rabbit and pig.

The Monkey

The monkey is intelligent and capable of using its wits to solve problems.

Monkeys often wriggle out of difficult situations and are not above trickery if it will further their own ends.

Monkeys tend to be oblivious to other people and to the effect their own actions may have on them.

In spite of this, they are usually popular and are able to motivate others by sheer enthusiasm for new projects.

Monkeys challenge, and their innovative approach and excellent memories generally make them successful.

They are full of energy and always active.

They have little sympathy for those who are unable to keep up with them, and will soon forget any difficulties.

Monkey is compatible with rat and dragon.

The Rooster/Cock

The rooster is a very sociable creature.

Roosters shine in situations where they are able to be the center of attention.

If a rooster is present, everyone will be aware of the fact because no rooster can ever take a back seat at a social gathering.

They are dignified, confident, and extremely strong-willed, yet they may have a negative streak.

They excel in arguments and debates.

Incapable of underhandedness, roosters lay all their cards on the table and do not spare others feelings in their quest to do the right thing.

They never weary of getting to the bottom of a problem; perfectionists in all that they do.

Roosters can usually be won over by flattery. Full of energy, roosters are brave, but they hate criticism and can be puritanical in their approach to life.

Rooster is compatible with ox and snake.

The Dog

The dog is entirely dependable and has an inherent sense of justice.
Intelligent, dogs are loyal to their friends and they always listen to the problems of others, although they can be critical.

In a crisis, dogs will always help and they will never betray a friend.

They can be hard workers, but are not all that interested in accumulating wealth for themselves.

They like to spend time relaxing.

Dogs take time to get to know people, but have a tendency to pigeon-hole them.

When they want something badly they can be persistent.

If roused they can be obstinate and occasionally they lash out, although their temper is usually short-lived.

Some dogs can be rather nervous and they may be prone to pessimism.

Dog is compatible with tiger and horse.

The Pig/Boar

The pig is everybody's friend.

Honest and generous, they are always available to bail others out of difficulties.

Pigs love the social scene and are popular.

They rarely argue and if they do fly off the handle, they bear no grudges afterwards.

They abhor conflict and very often will not notice when others are attempting to upset them. They prefer to think well of people.

Over-indulgence is their greatest weakness and pigs will spend heavily in pursuit of pleasure.

They always share with their friends and trust that, in return, their friends with make allowances for their own little weaknesses.

Great organizers, pigs like to have a cause and will often rally others to it as well.

Pig is compatible with rabbit and goat.

The Rat

The rat is an opportunist with an eye for a bargain.

Rats tend to collect and hoard, but are unwilling to pay too much for anything.

They are devoted to their families, particularly their children.

On the surface, rats are sociable and gregarious, yet underneath they can be miserly and petty.

Quick-witted and passionate, they are capable of deep emotions despite their cool exteriors.

Their nervous energy and ambition may lead rats to attempt more tasks than they may be able to complete successfully.

Rat is compatible with dragon and monkey.

Zodiac Animal Years

1	Ox
2	Tiger
3	Rabbit
4	Dragon
5	Snake
6	Horse
7	Goat, Sheep
8	Monkey
9	Rooster, Cock
10	Dog
11	Pig, Boar
12	Rat

Your birth year dictates your zodiac animal.

Take the last two digits of the year in which you were born and keep subtracting the number twelve until you reach a number less than twelve. Match that number to the list above, and you will find your matching animal. (e.g., 1980 would be: 80 minus 12 for 6 times (72) = 8 = monkey)

Good fun schway ... says Grannie!

Relationships and their problems need correction
in the bedroom in the Earth energy area which has become out of balance. Note the northeast and southwest corners for clues and clutter.

No junk rooms
are allowed. Good money is spent on storage. Difficulties can arise from
this if junk is located in the north sector; trouble in the career area will
appear. Junk in the northwest could affect friendships and travel.

Stress-free buildings
are those that are occupied with only things that are used, loved, and
needed. The rest must go. Make room for wealth to grow.

Refuse to multitask and improve your health and reduce stress
by allowing the energy to calm within and around you. Keep focused on
your immediate needs. Your inner energy will release creative ideas and
answers through inspired intuition.

Inspiration
comes during sleep. Bedrooms need balance and Yin and Yang
harmonized energy. Remove all stimulating items, such as electronics,
mirrors, and bright colors, so that good energy reaches you when sleeping.

Couples bed location
When sleeping together, the head of the bed (location) should face one
of the four best directions of the homes main 'bill payer'. (Personal
charts are calculated from the Pa Kua.)

The correct side of the bed
for sleeping is decided by the 'homecarer' (e.g., the man is a West
person so the location of the head of the bed is northwest. The wife is
an East person who picks her best side on which to sleep.). Everyone

benefits by being in harmony, as this important Relationship sector considers both individuals in determining placement,

Spiritual
Love and clothe the body well. Clarity forms from the positive energy of early morning nurturing and cleanliness.

Align your wardrobe
by colors (all whites together; blue tones together; red tones together, etc.) keeping color-harmony and balance with nature. It is calming to view and less chaotic.

Active positive energy
is made with music, candles, the ringing of bells, waving flags (movement), anything that makes you smile or laugh out loud.

Drenching pillows
in the sun reduces pain and headaches and produces powerful healing heat.

KNOWLEDGE

Command the forces of nature.

Feel the sun and believe,

Feel the earth and be relieved,

Touch the water and receive

The energy breath of the wind,

and

feel free.

Feng Shui movement of energy
warns of clogged and filled drains and must be kept clear for easy water flow, which helps to keep the lives of those in the building healthy.

Storage pieces
should be closed rather than left open, so as not to attract energy flow away from the meandering path.

Feng Shui warns of wet rooms that carry negative energy.
This includes all areas with bathrooms, toilets, open drains, kitchens, garbage, laundry, and dirt. These areas should be located in the occupant's worst four locations of their personal Pa Kua charts.

Positive energy can be encouraged
by keeping the drains plugged and toilet seats down at all times to prevent any financial energy from going down the drain, especially if these rooms are located in the wealth area of the building (always the southeast location).

Negative energy from bathroom and kitchen odors
can be corrected naturally with a vase of fresh flowers.

Wet rooms
should never be stimulated or activated with enhancements or other remedies in the wealth or relationship areas because this will only draw more negative energies.

University Lifestyle

Our vibrant olde city on the west coast, Victoria, accommodates a university, college, and numerous private schools and private colleges which overflow with students, providing a place with a vibrant pub life. A lot of graduates love the west coast for many reasons, and if their schooling happens to fit into their social life, all the better. We have had some fun with students and their new lifestyles.

Mark from Windsor, Ontario, and Marcia from Montreal, were spending an afternoon at the Royal British Columbia Museum. They were in a line-up for tickets for the Imax showing of a rock concert. We were among many waiting for the doors to open to the theatre. The couple was in line behind me and my friends, chatting about the great city they had discovered in Victoria. We loved hearing this, especially from those younger than seventy-plus. We had a brief conversation, advising them on some fun spots to visit.

It was early December, and Marcia explained that she wasn't looking forward to going back to Quebec for Christmas. She was rather enjoying the Mediterranean climate. They were living in an apartment near UVic campus and enjoyed being able to walk to classes.

The line-up into the theatre began to move. Mark explained his engineering studies were giving him some trouble. It was more than he had bargained for, and something else that he couldn't explain was bothering him as well.

There was a commotion in the back of the line. We turned to look. A broken escalator had caused havoc as fifty to sixty people began rushing around to find stairs. I commented, "Yuck. Negative energy!" The couple laughed.

"What's that all about?" they inquired with inquisitive grins. We started to move forward again.

I explained it wasn't great to be around things that were damaged, cracked, or broken. They stagnate positive energy. "And with all those people complaining, it doesn't help either," I said.

Marcia turned to Mark. "That must be it, Mark. Your room has a broken window, burnt out light, and God knows what all." She laughed.

As we entered the theatre, I said, "Don't laugh! It's true."

The Mick Jagger concert was fabulous. It was a great show that everyone enjoyed. A few of us went across the road to the Spaghetti Factory and had a bite to eat following the show.

Upon departing the restaurant, we walked to our parked vehicles. I was approached by the young couple I had encountered in the line earlier that evening. He was surprised that we had run into each other again as they had just been talking about me. Mark had wanted to know if I knew of anyone who might help with the setup of their apartment in regard to our earlier conversation. I quickly retrieved a business card and offered my services. (It just so happens, I had a few extra cards in my wallet.)

First thing in the new year, I was at their door with my bag of tricks, so to speak. The apartment was a really good size compared to small ones in all the newer towers that were being constructed in the city. However, it had probably been built in the early eighties and was due for a renovation.

I found that their corner unit was really bright, something that can give the overall atmosphere a good feeling. Lots of windows allow light into the unit. Still, there was something that bothered me. There was a sense of negative energy about the place; a hurtful feeling.

Marcia offered Mark and me a cup of green tea, and we walked through the unit. Mark was keeping pretty quiet about it all, as Marcia chatted about lack of storage. They had a lot of stuff for two students. Finally, I turned to Mark. It was his turn to comment.

Apparently, he had never felt comfortable in the suite. He was finding his studies harder than expected and just felt kind of down a lot of the time. I went into the room where he studied. He had set up in the second bedroom. There was a lot of stuff from computers, drafting boards, and books upon books stacked around the space. And the room did have a cracked window.

I didn't like the fact that he sat with his back to the door when sitting at his computer. I spent a few minutes suggesting ways to realign his studies. I wanted him to be situated in the Knowledge sector of the room, which was near the window, so he would receive good light on his work. I suggested going to Ikea for some needed storage shelves, and getting some of the backpacks and boxes into storage.

We organized the space while sipping tea. I told them they needed to get the window covered with anything, even a light sheer fabric, as I did not want to reduce the light into the room, but they needed to cover the damage until their landlord could get the window repaired.

We returned to the hallway, which was a bit dark. It was filled with numerous scattered pairs of shoes. I recommended they should place them on a mat in a controlled, limited space, so as to keep negative energy from circulating in the apartment. Heaven only knows what you might bring into the home from the bottom of your shoes.

There was definitely something hurtful about this space. It was as though the walls were vibrating with the need to be cared for. I could certainly understand why Mark had an uneasy feeling about the place. Your most powerful instinct is feeling the energy.

We visited the kitchen next. This was a deadly space. The cupboards had several broken handles. There were cracked tiles on the floor, and badly soiled, damaged countertops. This was totally negative energy. I wanted the whole room cleared out. We began from scratch and started making a list of things to do, such as getting some new dishes and getting rid of all the mismatched damaged items. Zellers was fine for making these purchases. I didn't care where or what they selected. They just needed to get some stability into the nurturing space. Everything was to be cleaned out, thoroughly. Repairs had to be made. It was time they called the landlord for some assistance. Even the knife-holder on the counter had to be placed out of view, as it represented weapons.

All cupboards had to be washed as well as all the windows and window sills. They also needed a mat on the floor by the sink to cover the cracked tiles until the landlord could attend to repairing them. A candle was lit during cleansing. The view from the window was the sharp edged roof of the next door building and had to be camouflaged with some kind of covering. There were things we could not change, such as the stove (fire element) which was situated across from the refrigerator (water element) and the sink. This is an area of huge negative energy, as water drowns fire. As long as they were aware of this, things would be a little better, but they were advised to never eat in the kitchen working area because of its state. They would find it much healthier to eat elsewhere. Arguments and mishaps follow bad energy.

We took a break in the living area of the apartment. Mark explained that they did not have a lot of choice when they moved in, because school was starting in only a couple of weeks. He said that he had just never felt comfortable living there. I wanted them to play detective and find out about the previous tenants. It might be interesting to hear why they had moved out.

I left them with a list of several things to move, clean, and be aware of. I told them that if it were at all possible, they should ask the landlord either to paint the unit or pay for the paint so they could do it. I left the recommended color chips and paint finishes to use.

In mid-February, Mark called my studio. He wanted me to drop by their apartment. He explained that he had done some research and found out that the last tenants had been living there about four months. They were a group of students crammed into the space. The tenants before them were an elderly couple that had lived there for over twenty years. The husband was apparently an alcoholic and very abusive. According to other tenants in the building, there were many fights and a couple of times the ambulance had to come to the unit. He suffered a stroke and was moved into a recovery unit, and the wife moved back to Seattle to live with her family.

I explained to Marcia and Mark that the space had probably never been cared for and all the incoming energy became negative. The hostile vibration was what Mark had sensed from the beginning of their stay. The environment lacked harmony. There was no sense of well-being. Mark felt his studies were suffering because of it.

When I entered the apartment once again, it was filled with flowers. The old furniture they had collected was situated on angles and was color coordinated with matching accessories, pillows, and throws. It was just the right amount, not overfilling the space. Every inch had carefully been tended to, painted, and fixed up. Greenery filled corners in wicker containers. There was now a sense of love that filled the space.

All windows had been covered with tab-top, floor-length, textured sheers, so not to hinder the incoming light but to hide the view. The older kitchen sparkled and all the repairs were completed; nothing was left out on the countertops. Even the knives, considered weapons, were tucked away behind a cupboard door. The new color scheme of parchment, white, and tan was soothing with touches of sky blue accessories. Mark was the first to comment that he actually felt good about his courses and that his marks were improving. They both felt nurtured and could feel the new positive energy change as they completed each task with care. It now felt like their home, with a little help from the landlord. The vibrations from the structure were now in harmony. The place had a nice feeling about it.

If you don't love your home, don't stay there. Never stay in someone else's negative energy. It only weakens your own good fortune. Be knowledgeable about how it feels. A building is also a living structure, vibrating with its own energy created by all those that built it, worked on it, lived in it. Create harmony and prosper.

Good fun schway … says Grannie!

The kitchen carries both positive and negative energies.
It is a space that nurtures and must be kept in harmony and balance to prevent arguments and mishaps, not to mention misfortunes.

Kitchens represent nourishment,
extending health and wealth. All the preparation surfaces should be cleaned with lemon and water solutions and be cleared of clutter, so as not to weaken the occupants' abundance.

Kitchens should be kept free from harmful chemicals
so as not to weaken the health of the occupants.

Well-stocked cupboards
with fresh-food items create abundance; but toss out anything not consumed or used over four months to open space for new abundance. Do not hold onto negative past energies, stale foods, and seasonings.

Yin and Yang in the kitchen
is accomplished by incorporating all the elements (five) by product, color, or shape. Examples:
White cabinets represent Metal color energy.
Stoves and ovens represent Fire element energy.
Tile floors represent Earth element energy.
Sinks and dishwashers represent Water element energy.
Greenery or wallpaper represents Wood element energy.
Rectangular islands represent Earth shape energy.

Feng Shui warns that mirrors in the kitchen only encourage
more fire and water, etc., which would be damaging to the energy balance of the space.

Kitchen islands
should contain or be constructed from an earth element when situated in the center of the room. Examples would be granite or tile surfaces. These surfaces should remain clear when not in use.

Excess Yin in a room
can be altered with natural sunlight, electric lights, or windows. When effectively used to expel the excessive Yin (dark corners), the light creates a more balanced space. Under-cabinet lighting in the kitchen is a must.

Health weakens
when the occupants eat in the kitchen working area or in any wet room, as this can add to poor health issues.

Kitchens operate best
when not located beneath other wet rooms, where negative energies are found to be pressing down on it.

Calming the kitchen
can be done by color coordinating countertops and back splashes with the same color, and by blending in the appliances (so as not to be easily identified) with cabinet fronts. This all helps to reduce visual clutter and energy flow confusion.

Kitchen and bathroom windows
are Fire elements and are should be kept clear and clean to encourage good health and prevent negative energy from entering.

High-tech kitchens
are designed for the gourmet cook; but if you live on fast foods, take-out, or small meals, opt for the juicer and sandwich grill, enhancing your finances for other luxuries.

Harshness
Don't cleanse a space with harsh chemicals that will kill off its positive energy; use natural products if possible, to reflect a caring, healthy home, and create a sense of well-being.

Wet rooms should be well-lit (even with the use of dimmer switches) and good under-cabinet lighting highlights food-prep areas and other counter spaces.

Kitchen calming
can be positive when some fun music is added to change the mood of the task when cooking or cleaning.

Feng Shui warns that the mouth of the oven should be oriented to the owners (bread-winners) best direction and should not point out the kitchen door.

Kitchens items stored, but rarely used
(less than four months) should be removed from the space, so as not to stagnate the energy. Keep cabinets filled with regularly used items and free from overcrowding. This stagnate energy is cause for confusion and poor memory.

Never cook or warm food
in any type of plastic container in the microwave. Plastic is a poison to your health and creates sickness and disease.

Nurturing kitchens
are ones that have no complications, clean appliances, and are well-equipped without malfunctioning items. Keep your burners spotless to prevent agitation and anxiety.

Harmful health energy
comes from off-gassing plastics that contain foods. Always place items
in glass (earth) containers or other natural elements to prevent unnecessary illness and irritability.

Containers made of plastic are especially bad for water
if left for any length of time where the sun can reach them. Water bot-
tles must not be in the sun.

Energy flow can be enhanced
by not situating a Water element (fridge) opposite a Fire element
(stove). This is to avoid drowning fires prosperous energies, bringing
unnecessary hardships and conflicting opinions and negative discussions.

Bathrooms are recommended to be located
away from the front entry. Placing them there means losing good
energy down the drain and weakening incoming friendships.

Bathroom mirrors
are never to reflect the toilet to avoid doubling the draining effect of
positive energy.

Bathroom negatives
are from toilets situated facing the entry door. Such placement only
encourages the negative energies to spread throughout the building.

Bathroom negative energies
should be kept separate from other areas with solid sound-proofing,
insulated walls constructed from concrete boards or similar products.

Orderly bathrooms
are ones with just the necessary toiletries that are used. Get rid of the
rest.

Never leave damp towels on the floor
as they suck up all the enhancing luck energy of the home.

Feng Shui recommends never having the head of the bed
against a wall where the bathroom toilet sits (on the other side). Such
placement can weaken the recovery of an illness, or cause one.

ATTRACTION

When searching for new ways to enrich your life,

be open to ideas that come to you

through mysterious means and uncharted paths,

from the unexpected

mystical movement of energy.

Aspirations for the workplace
The wealth area is the southeast area and a good place in the building
for an office. Client files within the sector enhance the space.

Along with an activation remedy
to enhance the energy of the Career sector; this could be accomplished
by placing a Water element fountain or fish tank next to a flowering
plant in a brass planter pot in the north section or wicker planter in the
southeast. A number of Asian restaurants will have such a remedy at
their entrance door.

Clutter in the Wealth sector
can enhance negative energy adding unnecessary debt and unwanted
anxiety. All invoices and bills should be covered or out of sight because
the energy will flow towards them, doubling their unwanted debt.

Wealth sectors (southeast)
can be diminished when white walls or white cabinets dominate the
space; the energy flow becomes still from any growth because white is
the color for Metal energy, which controls or cuts wood (the element
for southeast).

Work attitudes
affect your mood and this energy carries with you into other areas of
your life. If you don't love your work, make changes, as it will make a
difference to your environment.

Business intentions
are written and placed in your daytimer for new goals and successes to
be reached. Workers can also display agendas, goals, and intentions on
bulletin boards.

Financial Loss Reversed

Saturday was not a usual workday for me. I had gone into the studio to catch up on some last-minute prep work for an upcoming seminar on "Color Energy in the Workplace." I had just closed down the computer files, counted the required portfolios needed for the seminar attendees, and was about to lock up. I wanted some fun in the sun.

Loud stomping footsteps sounded on the staircase leading up to my studio on the second floor of a 1970s stucco building. A knock pushed the door ajar, and in stepped two middle-aged men sporting Levis and leather jackets, one carrying a large tan envelope. I recognized the shorter of the two. It was Ron, an artist I had worked with in Toronto many years before. I heard he had moved to the west coast a few years back, but I had never got around to looking him up.

We introduced ourselves once again. His cousin, Stew, was acting as chauffeur for him, being a native to the area. We chatted for a bit, catching up on each others whereabouts and happenings. Both men were familiar with my work in the energy field and Ron had consulted with me previously when planning his premises for his personal art shows. He was quite an accomplished artist and knowledgeable, as I had remembered, about classic Feng Shui applications. He had been prosperous in all of his endeavors. It wasn't long before he got to the point of his visit.

Ron understood the concepts of enhancing the Career sector of his building before any art showing. He was aware of the importance of energy flow into his space and the need to make sure positive energy complemented his personal Feng Shui charts. Even though he knew what to do, something was amiss. His dilemma was that he was broke and just couldn't get things right anymore. It didn't seem to matter what he tried, he couldn't get it to flow correctly.

When I assisted Ron, he was working in pastels, charcoals, and some oils. His pieces were peaceful, while others were quite energized, show-ing a unique talent to attract a varied market of purchasers. He had changed mediums and was now working in stone and marble sculptures.

Stew pulled open the envelope he had been holding and showed me several newspaper articles describing Ron's exquisite pieces, and lengthy columns praising his technique and creative images. Both were really puzzled because Ron's work had been accepted by the media, but were not selling at his showings.

I explained that I no longer had any of his personal records and needed to have his Energy charts calculated before I could view his workplace. He was planning a three-week showing beginning the following week. I told him I would do my best to get back to him no later than Tuesday, and we would meet again. I wrote down all the information I needed and we left it at that.

The following week, Ron's charts were ready. We met for a decaf at Mocha House in Cook Street Village and went over things. I could see he agreed with it all, but couldn't identify what he had missed when preparing for his shows and this puzzled him.

Ron had been working in his new art form for just over a year. It was about that time that his finances began to diminish. We headed over to his building.

He parked his van across the street from where he worked. The address was 2921; not bad, for his charts indicated he was a West energy person and the number two was prosperous, and all the address numbers totaled five (single digit total) which again was good for a West male. The energy flow into his building was the northeast direction (which also was just fine); indicating that the structure sat southwest, which also was perfect. The building was older and not as bright as I would have liked it to be, but it was well painted, with no chips or damage, and was in relatively good care. The studio was located on the second floor.

Ron unlocked the door to his space. The key worked smoothly, nothing sticking. He entered and I waited for a few seconds. I placed the compass at the entry. His space had an entry direction of west (good), but that meant his space would sit east. This was not great, as it would be classified as an East location for him. But, it did have fabulous natural light within the interior for his work from the windows. I spent a few minutes feeling out my first impression. His entry opened into the very large room. Something just didn't feel right.

Ron carried the energy of his birth year 1962 (Yang Water). There were some walls painted charcoal on the east and ivory on the north, which were both enhancing colors to the building's aspirations. Numerous spotlights highlighted his work; it appeared dramatic but also Zen-like with just the right amount of greenery in the south to enhance his personal recognition.

The large counter space for work was located in the Wealth sector of the room (southeast equals wood). It was well-lit and he would face northwest when sitting, which was good. The space was well organized and clean. A beautiful violet plant had been placed on the corner of his work desk. Ron's creative workspace was constructed from wood which was correct for this southeast sector, and his chair was covered in a natural woven fabric carrying all the colors of the elements in a small wave-like pattern. A large, framed watercolor (that he had painted) of the mountains around Whistler Village was situated behind the desk, providing him with good strength.

Ron's work area for carving the sculptures was located in his prosperous location, the west side of the room which is the Creativity sector. At first, I thought his back might be facing the entry door, but realized he had set it up correctly. He walked around throwing up his arms in disgust, exclaiming that he just couldn't get it. He felt it should be more prosperous. The old brick walls and wood floor added some character and did not show any damage from neglect. They had just aged beautifully. The energy flow in the space was meandering and without conflict.

All Ron's art and sculptures were displayed in the north (Career sector) of the room. He had always displayed his art in this sector. This was perfect when he was painting.

I raised a pointed finger and laughed out loud, then I pointed to the area. He shook his head, not understanding. I pointed directly, again at his art forms. He shook his head again. I walked over to the display area.

"Hello! The north section that carries Water energy is in the Career sector. North is Career everywhere, in every building, every city, and in every room. You know that. But, your work, these beautiful sculptures, is consistently an Earth element (stone)." I picked up an item admiring its beauty and precise detailing! Exquisite!

I said, "Earth dominates (dams) Water. Earth controls the energy of Water, and therefore will totally weaken and destroy the energy of this area which is the Career sector making it negative. This area was fine for your paintings, but these items need to be located in a sector holding the energy of Earth which would be the northeast sector or southwest sector of the room to attract positive energy."

Ron threw up his arms again, but this time smiling, understanding the theory. I explained that he was a Yang Water person. He was working with an Earth element (stone) that was only attracting negative energy into his life. It had nothing to do with his talent. He had correctly placed his work in the Career sector, which also was Water element, but the energy of the Career sector became weakened. He was totally amazed that he had missed the whole cycle of 'Elements: enhancement and control' theory. We both laughed hysterically as we realized the walls of his space were mostly brick, another Earth element that would resonate negative energy around him personally. He was just inundated with being and working in the wrong energy field and never caught on to it.

Another look at his space, and it was decided to make corrections by painting all the walls with a suede finish, silver-grey, leaving the texture of the brick showing. This would reduce the energy from Earth to Metal (color) energy which is the enhancement element for Ron. He installed numerous black platforms, shelving, and displays for his items, to bring Water energy (the color black) into his space. He relocated the display area for his sculptures to the southwest Earth sector. We added splashes of red to the South section (to promote his Recognition sector) with bouquets of red flowers and cushions for his black leather sofa. We also framed several newspaper clippings about his successes in black frames.

I encouraged Ron to rethink his medium, as the sculptures were beautiful, but truly not the best material for abundance and creating positive energy. Sometimes we just cannot see the forest for the trees, and we need to step aside and view our environment, listen carefully to our intuition, and create a balanced space filled with positive energy.

At his opening show, he sold over forty-five thousand dollars!

Good fun schway ... says Grannie!

Success
Crystals enhance when placed in the southwest or northeast locations.
Keep their energy prosperous in a west energy field. Nurture them by
cleaning them regularly, keeping them active by resting in the sun.

Success
can be encouraged by placing a group of red candles on a wood or green
tray, and locating it in the south sector of a south room. Always burn
the tips beforehand so they do not appear unused or neglected.

Lingbi stones (earth)
carry stronger energy when placed near candles or lamps (fire) in the
west, northwest and northeast sectors of a room to enhance ones
creativity, awareness, and knowledge.

Feng Shui recommends placing any personal recognition
on the south wall area. Examples would be diplomas, trophies, awards,
media print, photos, etc.

Placements
Support yourself with a high-back chair and a solid wall behind the
back of the chair when working, paying bills or being creative.

Powerful art such as mountains or towering buildings
all provide strength and always protect your back in a workplace or
study area.

Placement of the desk represents income,
prosperity and creative energies. The desk must be organized with all
papers contained and not scattered; bills and invoices should be kept out
of sight, so as not to draw additional debt.

Feng Shui warns to keep the energy positive
by removing anything cracked, damaged, or broken, even pens and
pencils, so as not to cause hardships.

De-clutter and dispose of all nonessential papers
for a clearer vision; out of sight, out of mind!

A subconscious energy drainer
is clutter, an unorganized space. Eliminate unnecessary files for clarity
and a new awareness opens up. Leave ten percent empty space for new
to enter.

Fire element
The desk and any work surfaces should have the fire present by being
well-lit. Good light from windows or lamps represents this element and
clarity.

Water elements should not be placed behind your desk,
including mirrors. Change any artwork if there are rivers, lakes, or pre-
dominantly black colors in it.

Energy flow
An office needs maneuvering ability for better creativity, thought, and
memory. Analyze the space carefully.

Fresh flowers
in the office, near or on the desk, attract growth when cared for regularly.

Your work
Write your intention and keep it somewhere in the sun, such as estab-
lishing a place of well-being and abundance and your goals.

Interior items need to be moved and touched
when cleaning so the whole space has been activated with positive
energy. Your mood must also be up. Break the routine.

Bad luck
in the Career area can be altered by placing two round stones in the
north area of your desk to dissolve or change it. (Earth controls water.)
Remove them once things change.

Trouble
in the Creativity sector (west) can be altered by placing red candles in
this space until the energy breaks and turns positive.

Bad working relationships
could alter with a dose of flowering plants placed in the southwest sector.

Recognition
Successes you have accomplished should be visually clear and located in
the south sector. Any good your profession has attained or business
accomplishments should always be available for others to see.

Don't locate your desk
under a window (fire element) unless the window has some sort of covering. Too much fire energy could lead to distractions, burn out, or lack
of focus.

Be specific when selecting furniture.
Too many wood elements are not suitable furniture choices for those
born in an earth energy year, so they do not feel that they are over-
worked and getting nowhere.

Beware of sharp corners
so that no poison arrows (protruding corners) face you or hit your back when working. This way you should not experience misfortunes, headaches, defective electronics, or anxiety.

Negative Business Discussions

Competition in business can be a stressful venture. One particular incident comes to mind.

In the fall of a very wet rainy season in Toronto, I was in the midst of finalizing an installation to a corporate headquarters lobby in the Don Mills area before heading to Rochester, New York, for the weekend.

Everything was near completion. The granite flooring, topped with colorful Tufenkian carpets, were cleaned for loose threads; the walls were covered in silk fabric-backed material; and the windows were topped with the latest Hunter Douglas product. The custom designed furniture was being placed as the artwork was installed, when I called out, "Whoops! Not there, Edward. That's not great Feng Shui." He rolled his eyes, smiling.

I felt an unexpected tap on my left shoulder from behind. Startled at first, I quickly turned only to gasp at the sight of the company's CEO smiling down at me. Oh, no! I thought to myself. He doesn't like it.

The scene changed from a hectic rush to silence. No one moved. He introduced himself, as if no one knew who he was, and invited me to follow him to his corporate office. No one made a sound as I shadowed the man down what seemed an eternal hallway to a private elevator. Within minutes, we entered a space that vibrated with the energy of grandeur. He offered me a seat in one of the cream leather sofas which focused onto a window with a view overlooking the valley. A silver tray sat on a black onyx table in front of me, holding a large Waterford crystal water pitcher. He poured two glasses of the sparkling liquid. He sat opposite me explaining that he heard my comment about Feng Shui moments before in the lobby. The CEO explained that he knew a little about the subject from his travels abroad over the years, but didn't really have an understanding about it. He wanted to know more.

A strong sense of relief settled over my whole being, as I realized that our meeting had nothing to do with the design of the new lobby. I cleared my throat as if I had some congestion when it was only a nervous reaction. I explained the concept of the mystical movement of energy and its effect on the environment, as well as our personal inner well-being. He listened attentively and had lots of questions.

His concern was that his tech company had numerous dealings with Asian countries, but they were losing a number of contracts. He wondered if the Feng Shui realignment could have anything to do with changing things for his company. I thought he must be asking because of a substantial decrease in sales. We spent a few moments discussing his many different business dealings.

The six-foot-two-inch man stood up and paced the office momentarily. He rubbed his hand through his thick, graying hair, then placed it into the pocket of his Harry Rosen suit. He explained that most business discussions took place in the building we were in and that everyone concerned would gather to discuss the details, product lines, deliveries, and availabilities of the items being negotiated. I suggested we go and take a look at the room where these meetings took place.

I wanted to know who and how many would be at an average meeting. He explained as we walked through the unusually wide corridors that they would have three visitors, but could, at other times, receive as many as five individuals. His company would have two or three representatives, executives, or managers from different departments attend depending on the situation.

We entered a well-lit room. My first impression was the room felt stagnant. The table needed to be turned the opposite direction and it would be better if it was an oval shape. He looked around the room observing my comments. The room lacked a life element as there was no greenery, limiting growth, plus it would help with the air quality control of the off-gassing from the synthetic carpeting in the enclosed space. I recommended a few large, round leaf plants in decorative ceramic pots for the southeast sector to enhance the finance area. Also, the large floor-to-ceiling windows covered two walls, a sign of vulnerability when not covered.

I excused myself to return to the lobby to get my briefcase and retrieve my compass. The four decorators rushed to my side to find out what was happening. I explained that it had nothing to do with our work. I sensed an air of relief from all as I quickly made my way back to the boardroom.

My second view of the boardroom didn't seem to enlighten me. The room was located in the northeast section of the building, which is the Knowledge sector of the building. This was an excellent space for discussions. (It could also do well in the northwest sector, a people and friendship sector.) The room needed an energy boost. I suggested a large red something on the center of the table. I recommended that it should be an item that he felt attracted to, for instance, a sculpture, bowl, or flowers, whatever he fancied. It was his business, and his energy was required. I suggested an Earth element to keep things grounded. The center section of any building, room, or table is earth. Granite tables and islands are an excellent solution for enhancement.

The space just didn't feel prosperous. I suggested that as the history of the company was very successful, perhaps a large photo of the company, or something to do with its history, should be situated on the west wall, enhancing the Creativity sector of the business.

Previous meetings, I was told, could last four or five hours depending on the size of the contract. I suggested to this handsome, tall gentleman, who showed keen interest in the matter, that it was important to have his people situated at the table in their personal best energy field, and facing one of their four best directions.

Each person has specific energy charts calculated from their birth year, detailing their positive and negative locations. Most Eastern or Asian individuals are aware of this factor and intuitively know where to sit. They would automatically situate themselves at a table in their most powerful energy field. The meetings that had taken place were conducted in such a matter that the guests were directed to the boardroom and allowed to enter and sit themselves first, followed by the company's executives. I suggested breaking this pattern. The CEO slipped a pen from his jackets inside pocket and jotted some notes down as I spoke.

We discussed the process further, and I was back in the lobby finishing the final touches of the job that I was originally hired for. With great interest, the four decorators and I soon departed to the nearest establishment for a few beverages and a needed meal.

He requested another meeting, where I recommended that his people allow the guests to enter as usual and have their discussions, but break the meeting for lunch. On their return to the boardroom, have his employees enter the room first, and sit down where the guests had previously sat, making sure that his executives were located in one their own positive energy fields. By doing this, it would break the energy flow, and confuse his guests, momentarily, attracting the incoming positive energy to themselves.

The earth's electromagnetic field affects each one differently. It's a fact of life.

After a few days, I heard back from the company with the birth dates of three people who would be in discussions with a potential new client. I completed their energy charts and met with each one individually for an overview of their auspicious locations to sit and directions to face to activate positive energy, then detailed the situation and how the process worked. The meeting was with a firm from Tokyo. I was told that if they bought the tech company's proposal, it would be a deal worth many millions of dollars.

Each executive knew exactly his or her best location to sit in the boardroom after their meeting broke for lunch, and they returned to complete negotiations. No one was to sit with his back to the entry door. No one was to face a protruding corner of a wall (pointed edge) known as a poison arrow as this alters the energy flow; its sharpness cuts the air, causing negative energy.

The room had been enhanced with natural elements and brighter upholstery on the chair coverings to incorporate all the colors of all the five elements to make sure nothing was lacking. The large windows had a control element installed, screen-blinds for protection, which didn't block out the light. They just controlled it to help reduce vulnerability.

The meeting took place and the Tokyo visitors entered the board-room first, with their coffees and portfolios, seated themselves and began discussions. The company's executives and managers noted their placements. The meeting resumed after their lunch break with the executives seating themselves first, in their new positions. They had entered, set their files down where their guests had previously sat, and situated themselves each facing one of their best directions taking in positive energy.

Their guests were confused at first by the energy change, as we all are when we return to a room where we once sat and find our seat taken by someone else. The executives resumed their negotiations in a new, compelling manner.

The success of situating the body in its correct energy field comes with good intuition and awareness. Because of this new understanding, I was rewarded well and they learned how to command the positive. The Tokyo company made their purchase, and the deal closed, in harmony.

Good fun schway ... says Grannie!

CLEANSING

Look closely around your exterior and interior.

Look closely at your inner thoughts.

Don't bring your past to the present

because it will dominate your future.

Why?

Throughout the eighties and nineties, the North American population was exposed to new technologies, new toys, new home decorating products, and more disposable income. The uncluttered home of the past became filled with things.

The more things, the more off-gassing from products, which causes the depletion of natural resources and elements. Eventually there is less spare time to organize these possessions resulting in a cluttered, unhealthy environment.

This new millennium demands new ways of looking at this issue and overcoming the complaints of the day, i.e., headaches, stress, disorder, feeling drained, and tiredness. When products in the office and home produce ill effects, it is time to analyze your surroundings.

EMFs (electromagnetic fields): both positive and negative energies flow freely in a healthy and prosperous environment.

Purpose of space cleansing.

To make healthy corrections to your surroundings which affect your career, wealth, creativity, health, and relationships.

To enhance your home and office with a sense of overall well-being and prosperity.

To produce a feeling of continuity and balance.

To create a space where you are productive,

To remove negative energy and fill the space with universal positive energy.

To create environmentally friendly interiors.

When to space cleanse.

Positive energy (chi) should gently circulate around the room like a meandering stream. Too much clutter changes the flow of healthy chi energy into negative sha chi energy.

As needless things are released and removed, (just like unwanted burdens, the load gets lighter) a new clarity is realized, in an energized space. If there is no space for the new to come into your life, then the old dominates and accumulates until an unhealthy environment develops.

The time to space cleanse is when you need correction in the areas of Career, Health, Relationships, Creativity, and Wealth.

The cleansing process revitalizes the space.

How to space cleanse.

Get a pencil and answer the following honestly.
1. Are your closets overfilled?
   With what?
2. Is there stuff behind doors?
   What kind of stuff?
   Why?
3. Are there boxes and things that haven't been used in several months?
   What's in them?
   How long have they been there?
4. Are there any shoes and things lying around the floors?
   Where?
   How many and why?
5. Anything stored under the bed?
   What?
   For how long?
6. Any clutter in the corners?
   What is it and why?
7. Any uncovered laundry baskets or trash cans?
   Where? (It could be in your romance area.)
8. Loose papers scattered on tables, floors, or furniture?
   Why?
9. Any things around you that you don't need, use, or love?
   Why?

Are all surfaces 50 percent clear of things?
11. Anything cracked, damaged, or broken?
  What and where are they?
12. Are there any stale aromas?

Select a closet first. Always record your answers.
Before starting, state your first impression. How does it make you feel?
Play music. (Sound is required at space cleansing time, and it should be
something that inspires you. Music you love.)
Keep a record of what music you played.

Procedure

Prepare a Space Cleansing Kit of your own.
You need all the natural elements in your presence (sample idea):
Fire: candle
Metal: plate, coins, or chain
Earth: pottery, granite, or crystal
Water: salted (ocean water is best)
Wood: bowl, twigs, cork, or a plant
Light the candle ...

Pour the salted water into the bowl, do not cover. Play music.

1. Remove everything from the closet.

2. Put all items into four different priority piles.

   Identify each item and sort as follows:

   a. things you use

   b. things you need, now or later

   c. things you love

   d. things to dispose of, the rest you give away

3. Throw away everything damaged, cracked, or broken.

4. If you haven't used an item in the past six months, then it probably should be in the 'd' pile. It is taking up space and accumulating old energies.

5. Have a bell to ring to stir things up, shake up stale energies, especially in corners.

6. Do a thorough dusting and vacuuming of the space.

7. Wash down the walls.

8. Make any required repairs to the damaged areas.

9. If a stronger correction is required, then paint the space in an enhancing color in latex paint.

10. All hangers should match in a closet and be the same color.

11. Put back only things that are used, needed or loved, in an organized fashion.

12. Place items together in color sections.

13. Nothing is to be on the floor; shoes on racks, in boxes, or placed on shelves.

14. Always have empty hangers and open space (ready to accept new).

15. Add fragrance or eucalyptus.

16. Light fixture must always be in good repair.

EVERYTHING SHOULD APPEAR SPACIOUS, NOT CROWDED OR CRAMPED.

For maximum correction it is vital to your health to consider the removal of all off-gassing plastics, synthetics, materials, and products containing volatile chemicals (especially in children's rooms).

Exercise:
   Name three areas where you spend the majority of your time.
   Example would be:
      Bedroom: 8 hours
      Kitchen: 4 hours
      Home office: 6 hours

   1. _____
   2. _____
   3. _____

Element Enhancement

These three areas that you have selected are the rooms you should apply enhancements and/or controls, new furniture realignment, color analysis, and accessorize after a complete space cleansing.

Results: You will sense a feeling …

- motivated
- clear headed
- less burdened
- revitalized
- content
- balanced
- healthier
- rested and relaxed
- focused
- cheerful and upbeat
- positive attitude
- rested and sleep better
- independent
- self confident
- behavioural changes
- removed energy blocks
- everything seems balanced
- a sense of well-being
- *ready to conquer life's challenges, again.*

You will achieve the best results by observing and developing the ability to survive and thrive with nature by removing negative energy, and by giving room for universal, positive energy.

Nature is a delicate balance of all elements constantly interacting with each other in a continuous cycle of creation.

Go with the flow and be in harmony with your environment.

WISDOM

All energy sources comes from the power of the sun
Which has accumulated in the earth.
Light inhaled by plants,
Buried in coal, mineral fields;
Converts water into vapor then to rain or snow
Which is released back into the earth.
No life of any kind can exist without sun energy
As it is the source of life itself,
Animal, vegetable, and mineral.

Be there, where you are to be.
Speak, when you are to speak.
Beware!
You are there, consciously.

*   *   *

Be in the moment
Look around your environment
Yesterday is today past
Tomorrow is today future
They are all, today now
Do what you need to do ... now.

*   *   *

The dragon energy within
is an indication of coming to terms
with one's passions and chaotic beliefs
in order to become a custodian of one's own future.

*   *   *

Change is our ability to grow!
Burn off negative energy
with regular, daily, physical exercise.
Moderate your emotions for clarity.
The eye of the construction,
the peak of the pyramid
is the element earth center.

*   *   *

This area of a building or room should remain clear of obstruction.

*   *   *

The cornerstone of a building is the *living heart* of its foundation.

*   *   *

A strong, well-fed, rested body has a sharp memory and mind.

*   *   *

The flow and balance of natural energies
lies hidden between
(feng) wind on earth = the breath of the body within.
(shui) water on earth = the body of humans within.
A relationship with the environment is created
when the planet and your body are harmonized and in balance.

*   *   *

Before you begin any activity, always start by enhancing positive energy
in and around you with three very deep breaths.
Inhale into the stomach making it expand; then tightening it as you
exhale.
This will always bring your senses into a clear awareness state.

*   *   *

Ancient cultures
would cleanse by placing the flat palms of their hands over ears firmly
then quickly release ten times.

*   *   *

Fly a flag
with your desires of giving and receiving written on it
is a very powerful affirmation.

*   *   *

Healing water
(drink whenever and as much as possible)
was considered that which had rested in an earth container (glass)
in the sun for three hours.

*   *   *

Everyone sees you differently.
A student, a neighbor, a gardener, a teacher, a parent,
a child, a romantic, an athlete, a sister, a boss, a sailor, a grandfather ...
All have very different personalities.
List twenty-five different identities you have had since childhood.
Contemplate these different energies as positive or negative.
The Yin and Yang usually balances out.

*   *   *

Break routine.
Always walk, drive, travel a different way to work
to renew energy and stimulate the visual.

*   *   *

An observer's energy can influence an experiment.

*   *   *

You can't do tomorrow, what you can do today,
when your passion and energy is at its peak.
Time just passes you by.

QUESTIONS AND ANSWERS

THE MYSTICAL MOVEMENT OF ENERGY

BRUSHES ACROSS YOUR CHEEK,

TAPS YOU ON YOUR SHOULDER,

RAISES THE HAIRS ON YOUR ARMS,

RUNS CHILLS UP AND DOWN YOUR SPINE,

NEVER TO BE SEEN.

THE MYSTICAL MOVEMENT OF ENERGY.

My family consists of me and my dog. I have moved to a new home and find that he is very restless and doesn't seem to want to settle down.

Animals have strong instincts. He is obviously not comfortable. Animals also have positive energy fields, and when they find the right room and can lie around for hours, you know they have found it. My cat would lie on a small wicker chair I had in the bathroom while the dog would lie anywhere he could find in the sun. We are all happier when we find our best locations. Unless the home is carrying negative energy that he senses, he will eventually settle.

Should I buy some tassels to activate the energy and put a turtle in the north for career enhancement?

Unless you were born with an Asian background, we don't have this following in our culture. Less is best to activate a change in energy, so that the energy can reach your desires. Place what you want to happen in your career (north) sector either with photos, or books, or written affirmations; and the enhancements are black and white or metal and water items and nothing else. Pink light bulbs, tassels, and dragons are not North American enhancements.

I'm in school still, and am having a terrible time with one of my subjects which I have to get to graduate.

The knowledge sector is the northeast area of a room which is a good place to keep your texts. Keep your desk clear of other subjects. Pay attention to where you are actually studying this subject. Are you sitting elsewhere or lying down? You could be in one of your negative spaces making it impossible to grasp. You also need to do deep breathing before studying as you must relax to absorb the knowledge. Also, chat with another student who does well in it. I recommend a large red candle when studying, which sits in the northeast area.

I have a bachelor condo and need assistance. How do I begin?

Take a compass and align it with the entry door to see what energy the condo carries. Does this match your energy which you carry from your birth year? (e.g., east/west building to an east/west person) Your energy charts will provide you with a Pa Kua number and your best location for your bed, dining area, office, or TV area. You use these locations to set up your furnishings. What is your first impression when entering? Does the space talk to you? Does it feel good to you?

What is my first consideration before buying or renting?

Regardless of the decor, does the space *feel* good to you?
Is there good sunlight within the structure?
Ask yourself if you could live there for several years?
Is there adequate space for your lifestyle?
What appears to be damaged or broken that needs fixing before you relocate?
How many sharp corners, overhead beams, or hanging lights are there?

I love our new house, but my partner doesn't feel the same way.

Your partner's inner intuition is warning him of something negative. You should investigate the previous owners and find out why they sold it. Was there a financial problem or illness? There may be some bad energy left from the previous owners which could easily be corrected with an interior realignment once it is specified.

My new office building faces directly onto an oncoming road. I don't like this feeling of one day being crashed into.

Your intuition is correct. Your home or business can suffer harsh, negative energy entering the premises in this type of situation. Some suggested corrections are:

- a curved or meandering entrance way

- a large protective stone, or landscaped enclosure or fence

- the entry door to be recessed and installed on an angle to divert this strong, incoming energy

- tall, beautiful flowering plants on each side of the door

- a protective covering over the entry door, or a solid wood door

- an octagon-shaped mirror placed outside (centered) above the main door reflecting this harsh energy away.

The garden around my front entrance is a disaster as nothing we are planting works in the north in this soil.

Nurse the soil for three weeks to three months. Redesign the space with limited flowering shrubs and consider creating a container garden where you are in control over the elements. Plant numerous seasonal flowers, but all to be in one color, white. (This is a Metal color which enhances the north sector of the home.) Try and select round leaf shrubs and plants over spiky leaf ones.

We have recently downsized and are now living in a town-bungalow and find it very dark because we are located in the middle of a section of six units.

Living in a row house situation needs special attention to brighten and enhance the atmosphere. Consider light walls on the sides and a deeper shade on the end walls, with contrasting furniture such as tan-colored furnishings. Keep wall-colored, floor-length drapery on dark rods with textured fabric, and add dark framed artwork; but keep the floors light. This Yin and Yang color combination keeps the energy meandering and positive. Keep a splash of red in the south, northeast, or southwest.

My sister drives me nuts with her dozens of shoes all over the place that never get put away.

Shoes protect us from harmful matter and disease. You just never know what they have picked up along the way, and unless they are kept in your control, on shelves, mats, or in boxes, the energy they have picked up resonates throughout the space. This shoe clutter can create anxiety, arguments, even laziness, as well as anger when not being under your control. You can only wear one pair at a time, so the rest should be organized, cared for, and a special place created for them, out of sight. No need for unnecessary havoc.

My job keeps me busy, and I am having difficulty with the constant pick-up of kids' toys all the time.

Children like to copy others. If they see a tidy, organized room, and are shown that they have a special place for their things, that is strictly theirs, they tend to learn at a young age. Your environment is a reflection of how others treat you. Have chairs or foot stools that can be opened for their own storage. Their room could also be carrying too much energy from a strong color and lots of stuff around. Calmer surroundings help with their studying, creativity, sleeping, and listening. Like attracts like.

I live in the tiniest place on this planet. I can't even find a place for the ironing board which is used most every day.

The iron is Fire energy and is not meant to be left out. Be creative and make a funky cover for the ironing board and hang it on the wall, like a surfboard or unique photo board. It will then turn into something that is loved and the negative energy will turn positive. We all have things we use daily that need to be left close by, but make sure it is organized and not showing unfinished work which could be just laziness. Storage baskets, wall units, and furniture that contain storage are a great investment. The flow of positive energy is an important fact of life, not to mention, good fun schway, the North American way!

978-0-595-48273-3
0-595-48273-2

Printed in the United States
108697LV00003B/160-237/P